http://twitter.com/eugager

http://eugager.tvgio.com

PREFACE

Our democracies use outdated technologies.

Is the internet the biggest test tube for how technology shapes society?

How technology shapes society?

Examples arise from the internet.

Blogs/ wiki/ slashdot...

Each of those defines a different society.

The 21st Century Democracy?

Roads Crossed

GS > Back in 2005, at a company called ParTecs (Participatory Technologies), I started working in a research project for an e-democracy and collaborative deliberation platform which started in 2001. Its creator, Rufo Guerreschi, had the idea after the first World Social Forum in Porto Alegre (the city in which I was born). The project had many ups and downs and never became commercially available. The company was sold, pieces of the software were released as Free/Open Source Software and most of the ideas were inherited by the Telematics Freedom Foundation, a non-profit created to promote e-Democracy and the combination "Freedom+Privacy+Security" in communications for every world citizen.

In 2007, the ideas recycled from the old platform shaped a Telematics Freedom' project proposal called Do2Gether (part of a wider program called "Continuous Democracy"). Basically, a Political Social Networking website.

By November 2008, it came to my knowledge that there was an European call open for "ICT for Governance and Policy Modelling" due on April 2009, and one of the target outcomes was a "Governance and Participation Toolbox". Perfect match and evolution for DoGether. I promptly invited some people that could be interested in the same arguments, and after about four months of work we came out with the proposal which you are about to read in this book.

PSdF > Two questions were going around my mind for some time before embarking in co-writing this proposal. The first was: "how will 21st century going to be like?". And the second was: "how does technology defines the way the society emerges?". Of course the two questions were heavily intertwined.

The first question was inspired by a conversation with my father, Donato Speroni, a retired journalist who loves his work too much to stop researching and writing. He observed how the democracies we have in the west have, by and large, been designed in the 18th century. With the technology of the 18th century. The reason why in the US, for example, the presidential elections were designed as indirect elections, with the voters choosing an electoral college who then would vote for the president was mostly for logistical reason. With the members of the electoral college voting more than one month after to permit to them to reach Washington by horseback. Similarly in Ireland the parliament only meets two days a week because in the old times each week they would go back to the province that elected them, to report on what has happened (again on horseback). Although none of this happens today, the structure has not changed much in the meantime.

The second question came to me as I was observing the birth of web2.0. By looking at the birth of Livejournal, Delicious, several blogs, Wikipedia, Slashdot, and many others I could see how different technologies would spur different type of social interaction. Depending if the users were able to communicate to each other, could do this privately or could start a personal thread inside the comments on a post, the relation between them would change. And as this changes would happen over and over again (provided the technology would permit it), society itself would change. The most clear example for me was the blog of the Italian comedian Beppe Grillo. The most followed blog in Italy, with on average more than a thousand comments for each post. But with very limited possibilities for commentators to contact each other. Thus creating in general a huge support for the political activities of the comedian, but very little possibilities for his supporters to split into sub groups that could more easily focus on particular issues (or criticize him). The changes that would be necessary to make this happen would be very tiny. But the effect on a socio-political level (among the million people that support him) would be huge.

As the two questions came together, and started interacting, I was naturally drawn toward thinking, and imagining, how should we design a democracy for the 21st century. As part of this quest I first joined the group metagovernment (metagovernment.org), I gave a talk in Zurich on the topic "How should the 21st century democracy be organised?"

and finally agreed to join efforts with Giovani and his newly formed team to write a grant proposal on the topic.

- - -

So how is 21st century democracy going to look like? The EUGAGER proposal to the EU 7th framework programme tried to answer that question or, at least, build the first block of a truly collaborative and secure platform where Governments can deploy their web applications, while providing their citizens with a place to interact freely.

And because the European Union is still to conceive such a platform many groups on civil society are working on it.

Some enlightened politicians are trying to push for more integration between internet and bureaucracy. In the meantime normal citizens with "more-than-average" web skills (i.e. hackers and geeks) are going the other way, trying to build a bottom-up application that would let (a) a group of people to self organize and (b) scale well with size. Each of them is hitting a different wall. The politicians are hitting the wall of privacy. Privacy laws are particularly strong in the EU, and require the governments to be unable to know so much about the voters (citizens) sensitive data. On the other hand, hackers are hitting a very different wall. The wall of authority. First of all, a non-official web service will never have the authority to define what the next decisions of the government should be. Also, the people who participate in those web services are never representative samples of the population. Usually the people who participate are people interested in the topic, activists, and people directly involved. None of those representative of the society at large.

With EUGAGER we tried to provide an answer to both problems. Privacy would have been dealt by splitting the information about users between the main platform and each application. Only a person administering both could try to recover the information, but not without tricking the Security API. Authority is of course answered by the endorsement of the EU and its Member States in using it to launch or migrate their e-participation sites.

We noted that where governments actually fail to tackle their citizens' needs, proprietary platforms like Facebook succeed in gathering groups of people and stimulating them to participate, even if with lower level of identity verification, security and trust on results... And in the meantime, our colleagues in the US are discussing very similar ideas on having the "Government as a Platform"...

The story does not obviously end here.

GS - Giovani Spagnolo
PSdF - Pietro Speroni di Fenizio

The following persons have collaborated to write the original proposal
(in alphabetical order)

Armin B. Cremers

Chris Anderson

Donatella Piccinin

Enrico Tronci

Federico Mari

George Velegrakis

Giovani Spagnolo

Igor Melatti

Ivano Salvo

Luigi V. Mancini

Natassa Kazantzidou

Panos Katsambanis

Pietro Speroni di Fenizio

Rufo Guerreschi

Sofia Spiliotopoulou

Stefan Lüttringhaus-Kappel

Tobias Rudorf

Xenia Chronopoulou

Small or medium-scale focused research project (STREP) proposal
ICT Call 4
FP7-ICT-2009-4

EUGAGER - An Open, Secure and User-Verifiable Web Platform for E-Governance and E-Participation

Small or medium scale focused research project (STREP)
Date of preparation 31/3/2009
Version number 1

Work programme topic addressed:
Governance and Participation Toolbox

Name of the coordinating person: George Velegrakis

Partic. no.	Participant organisation name	Partic. short name	Country
1 (coord.)	AINTEK A. E.	IDEC	Greece
2	Sapienza University of Rome	UNIROMA1	Italy
3	Telematics Freedom Foundation	TFF	Italy
4	University of Coimbra	FCTUC	Portugal
5	TurnFront	TESIA	United Kingdom
6	University of Bonn	UBO	Germany

Proposal Abstract

The evolution of the Internet from static content to user-oriented, dynamic services involves new challenges and opportunities.

In this context, the EUGAGER project consists of research, design and prototype implementation of a web-based, open and secure toolbox for e-government and e-participation tools.

The proposed system will consist of a core (toolbox) providing a basic set of secure primitives (an open Application Program Interface) including those typically needed for the design of complex e-governance and e-participation web applications (tools). Moreover, the toolbox will support external tools resting on the toolbox API. The proposed system will enable project stakeholders (governments, SMEs, non-profit organizations and existing e-participation/e-government free/open source communities) to make the system evolve by creating new tools and eventually constitute an ecosystem for citizens engagement.

Citizen engagement will be greatly encouraged by EUGAGER. Indeed, it will provide: 1) advanced and usable tools for knowledge learning, interpretation, sharing and creation; 2) a flexible authentication mechanism ensuring privacy; 3) trusted tools that allow citizens to verify that their inputs are correctly taken into account in application results.

On the other hand, EUGAGER will be a powerful tool for governments: 1) powerful knowledge filtering helps governors to meet citizens will; 2) certified secure API ensures the toolbox against misuse and malicious attacks. Moreover, planned case studies dissemination and exploitation will increase government awareness about ICT impact on democracy. The involvement of the Italian Government (Presidenza del Consiglio dei Ministri) in the EUGAGER project will allow to put the foundations for a wide European collaboration, also stimulating other governments to join the network, thus enlarging the community of EUGAGER platform users.

Table of contents

1 SECTION 1 - SCIENTIFIC AND/OR TECHNICAL QUALITY, RELEVANT TO THE TOPICS ADDRESSED BY THE CALL

1.1 *Concept and Objectives*

1.1.1 Motivations

The Internet has shown the rise of a series of emerging communities thrived on different technologies (blogs, wiki, discussion groups, social software, etc.). The evolution of the World Wide Web from static content to user-oriented, dynamic services involves new challenges and opportunities.

E-government should be the area in which government and common citizens are able to interact. Since the beginning of the US Presidential Campaigns the interest of regular citizens in the way governments work and treat citizens' feedback has largely increased. In particular, political engagement via Internet is becoming mainstream as citizens increasingly contribute opinions or ask questions to their government representatives or help fund causes they support (as the famous Obama Funding Campaign which attracted millions of dollars from small donors) [W:dfnh-web].

Unfortunately, many governments are not aware of how they can use these new technologies and reach critical mass to have quick feedback on policy-making processes. Moreover, there is a lack of tools that permit common citizens to voice their opinions, find different opinions, integrate their different opinions, endorse the opinions they agree on, and respond to the government in a unified manner to questions posed to them. The lack of available technologies and awareness and on these themes is however outweighed by the huge interest shown by European Governments about these subjects. Italian government (Presidenza del Consiglio) has declared its interest in this project and it will actively participate to Dissemination and Exploitation phases.

EUGAGER aims to cover this gap by providing a base platform with a single user-base for the creation of e-participation and e-governance tools: EUGAGER aims to design and implement the necessary tools for authentication and identification, knowledge acquisition, retrieval and filtering and citizens participation in government decision-making process.

The EUGAGER platform will be built upon a suitable set of formally certified primitives which increase transparency while ensuring privacy and security.

Knowledge manipulation. The evolution of the World Wide Web from static content to user-oriented, dynamic services involves numerous opportunities and challenges for information retrieval and filtering. Content based search engines belong to the everyday life and probably pose a big contribution to the success of the web. The more users participate actively in online communities nowadays, the better collaborative approaches may succeed. Personalized search and filtering is possible by absorbing basic social activities such as mouth-to-mouth-propaganda in online communities instead (or in enhancement) of using strictly content based techniques. A big advantage of collaborative approaches is the possibility to abstract away from the content by using human intelligence in form of ratings to create new (meta-) information. EUGAGER will provide the European community with the necessary platform to do this. The users' ratings also define a profile by which he is comparable to other users. Similarity measures between users can be defined and used for creating a neighbourhood graph and clustering as well.

The user must be able to handle comfortably the high (and growing) amount of content that EUGAGER will contain. Users may add applications, comments and other content which might be too much to browse manually for others. Of course there will be content which is interesting for (nearly) everybody in the European community, but one can still expect applications, documents and other content to only concern a   smaller part of the community. The growing of the community is one of the most important aims and it is endangered if users are frustrated by too much content without some kind of help which shows them the content which they are personally interested in.

Getting statistical information on a big community is, in general, very interesting and if the user gets something in return he might be more interested in sharing his knowledge. We can provide the user with more personalized help if he contributes more to the system. On the other hand, this higher contribution leads to more statistical data of the

European community. This is a win-win-situation that EUGAGER will provide in trustworthy and secure way.

The anonymous statistics of the system may also help the scientific community to evaluate existing and new recommender systems.

Security. Appropriate security measures are essential prerequisites for e-government platforms. As with any technical system, a system of this kind may be exposed to errors and deliberate or unintended attempts to circumvent security measures. In this context, moreover, the criticality of the subject poses even more key security requirements to be addressed and assured. Attacks need to be prevented and particular attention needs to be paid to possible systematic attacks, as these can particularly affect results and transparency of the entire process. The platform architecture has to be designed to assure an adequate level of security and to guarantee the properties of confidentiality and integrity of information, identity and access control, privacy of users.

In order to cope with security issues in a distributed and evolving scenario, we need flexible specification languages. Usually flexibility and expressiveness come at the cost of complexity and lack of desirable-property enforcement. Often, common properties for specific access control policies may not be satisfied due to unforeseen interactions among rules or sequence of rules and cooperation of agents: this may lead to discrepancy between what the policy authors intend to specify and what they actually formally specified. This motivates the use of formal verification tools to prove required security properties.

Transparency. The main objective of this project is to empower and engage all types of societal groups and communities, enable them to utilize mass-cooperation platforms and allow governments to incorporate their input while safeguarding against misuse. We think that this will be possible through the availability of platforms and tools that are able to prove that they are fully transparent and that allow users to verify how policy-makers take their decisions. Citizens should have the assurance that their inputs are taken into account by their governors. The transparency has to be in some way bidirectional: governors, by their side, should be assured that users' identity is fully verified and no misuse is allowed. In addition, users are always more worried of preserving their privacy and security, and these are the key features that this project will address. We think that designing and developing such a platform will allow citizens to trust their administrators more and will help the policy making process to be more adherent to citizens' will.

1.1.2 Objectives

The main goal of this project is to build an extensible, secure and transparent web platform (or toolbox) for e-participation and e-government tools. The platform will also provide the functionality of collecting, learning and synthesizing knowledge coming from a broad folksonomy, i.e. the practice and method of collaboratively creating and managing tags to annotate and categorize content.

We also aim to define a general framework, which allows both i) the governments to build trusted application (by relying on platform services) and ii) any citizen to develop tools for e-participation, as well as to define new services to be used by other user-defined tools.

We will also give examples of e-participation and e-government tools relying on our platform.

1.1.2.1 Knowledge

Recommendation system. We will provide the user with personalized recommendations based on his profile, comparable to recommender systems such as the ones in Amazon or lastFM. But unlike these examples we do not know anything in advance about the content the users will add to EUGAGER. This is why the recommender system has to be flexible in this regard. We will provide different kind of dimensions the user may choose from to get recommendations. E.g. he may search for content he agrees to or content he is interested in. This is not necessarily the same: a citizen does not have to agree to or like a proposal to find it interesting or important and therefore get it recommended, but on the other hand he should agree to or like an application to get it recommended.

By letting the user choose which dimensions are important for every search, we provide him with the necessary flexibility to filter new content of EUGAGER in different ways. Of course, we will also offer predefined templates for standard filtering problems and the possibility to create and share such search profiles in the community.

Tagging system (Knowledge learning and tracking). As citizens input their opinions on the net, we need to produce a search tool that permits them to efficiently retrieve existing opinions. This is to avoid dispersing their efforts through many different, but equivalent, opinions. And this is also to see different opinions on a topic, with the aim of integrating part of them, to gain a wider endorsement. There are many ways to produce such a search tool. Our aim is to use a bottom-up approach, which results in an organization of the information that mirrors the culture of the people that are using them.

We should thus produce three separate, but intertwined search tools. Each opinion that has been inserted should be linked with related opinions. There should also be a search box, where the user can search directly all the opinions inserted, and finally the opinions should be clustered in topics of knowledge. Those topics of knowledge should be emergent from the opinions inserted, and from the keywords inserted by the users. As such, the way they will appear will mirror and give information on the group of people that generated them.

Knowledge synthesis. Citizens need to be able not only to voice their opinion, but also to endorse each others' positions; to synthesize them into a coherent whole that takes into consideration different, but equally valid, points of view. From an IT perspective the aim of this process is to let people search in the space of possible opinions, looking for the opinion with the widest possible endorsement. To achieve this goal we want to produce a Darwinian system of knowledge. In a Darwinian system the evolution is generated by subsequent evaluation of existing partial solutions, and productions of different mutations based on them. Such mutations are effectively searching the space of possible solutions to a problem.

1.1.2.2 Security

The objective is to realize a layered architecture, based on a safe, reliable and trustworthy toolbox, that will be designed to assure an adequate level of security and to guarantee the properties of confidentiality and integrity of information, identity and access control, privacy of users.

The toolbox will be designed considering security issues from the beginning, instead of following a common approach of adding security mechanisms to an already existent software architecture. In fact, the experience/statistics shows that the latter approach results in a weaker system where the added security mechanisms can be often easily bypassed.

It should be formally proven (verified) that the proposed system does have the above properties, notwithstanding malicious attacks (misuse). On top of this trusted toolbox, high level applications will be designed and realized, using the primitives (to be identified in the research project) provided by the trustworthy layer. A first objective is to guarantee a home-banking level security, focusing of new methods of authentication and access control, on the definition of strict policies and the verification of software to guarantee the overall web application security.

It is worth noticing that putting together secure components does not usually lead to building a secure system. Even though many security technologies exist, they usually address one or more single element of a system or, even worse, just one security property (e.g. only integrity or confidentiality). A more general framework is necessary to deal with a complex architecture such as the one needed in a context of participation web platforms.

Formal verification. Since security is such an issue when dealing with e-government applications, it is important that the security protocols devised to cope with attacks and misuse are carefully verified to be sound.

We thus plan to use model checking techniques to mathematically certify that the security protocols we will use in this project indeed prevent attacks and misuse. To the best of our knowledge, this is the first time that model checking is applied to e-government issues.

Moreover, we plan to go a step further when dealing with the problem of defining a control access policy avoiding misuses and attacks. In fact, we aim to be able both to formally verify given control policy rules, and to automatically synthesize access control policy rules starting from a high level specifications.

Granular privacy management. Luxury cars today offer something called a "valet key". It is a special key you give the parking attendant and it prevents them from driving your car more than a few kilometres, opening the trunk, or accessing your onboard phone address book. The idea is pretty straightforward. You give someone limited access to your car with a special key, while using your regular key to unlock everything.

Everyday new social networking websites offer services which tie together functionality from other sites. But the implementations available today request for your username and password to the other site to be able to connect. When you agree to share your secret credentials, not only do you expose your password to someone else, but you also give them full access to do as they wish. They can do anything they wanted – even change your password and lock you out.

We will solve this problem by implementing the EUGAGER Authentication and Tool Manager, which will allow the User to grant access to his private information on EUGAGER, to available tools (Petition and Collaborative Proposals). With this approach, many existing e-participation sites, created by citizens or officially supported by governments, will be able to interact with the EUGAGER core components with a few code additions.

1.1.2.3 Transparency

Once governments commit to strategies transforming their governance processes, significant challenges and opportunities will arise during their implementation process. Among design challenges, transparency is one of the most remarkable [M:e-gov].

In [M:e-gov] is noted how citizens should be able to understand government decisions. A lack of transparency could prevent the public from actively participate in common decisions, and can easily conceal favouritisms.

Moreover, distributed applications do not generally ensure the user of the correctness of the results. A tool could retrieve data and then post process it in an arbitrarily malicious way, easily cheating an unaware citizen.

Our aim here is thus to implement the toolbox in a way preserving transparency, by following the principle of Minimum Trusted Computing Base. In particular, one of the recommendations we want to follow is to give citizens (users in our context) the ability to check the results of all applications lying on the toolbox. To this aim we will develop a certified trusted tool for both data and tool results verifiability.

1.1.3   Approach

Our aim is to design a secure, transparent and knowledge-based platform, combining both extensibility and scalability. The platform will be extensible meaning that users—citizens, governors and companies—are allowed to propose their opinions or endorse existing ones. Moreover, the platform will be scalable, permitting special users—governors and companies—to design new applications lying on the trusted core, the toolbox.

In the following sections we will describe how we intend to give knowledge learning and creation a predominant role (Sect. 1.1.3.1), how we will secure the system from malicious attacks (Sect. 1.1.3.2) and the mechanisms we will apply to oblige applications to supply the users with correct results (Sect. 1.1.3.3). Finally we will give implementation insights (Sect. 1.1.3.4).

Our contributions will be applied to a concrete framework, called EUGAGER.

1.1.3.1 Knowledge

In order to make knowledge the predominant force entailing decisions, we will design a *multidimensional collaborative recommender system*, which offers to the user multiple personalized possibilities to filter EUGAGER's content. It will be necessary to create user profiles, which contain the user's ratings for items on multiple dimensions such as interest, agreement and importance. This allows statistical analysis of opinions and personalized filtering of new and existing content so that the user can be informed of new documents or applications, which concern him in different ways. The variable types of rating must be analyzed and classified either manually (if possible in advance) or by statistical analysis of the user behaviour later (like modern search engines adjust from time to time to the user behaviour).

Even if peoples´ opinions are often diverse there are types of ratings, which are more objective than others. E.g. most people would agree that a text containing swearwords is malicious in a political discussion. An opposite example would be the rating of a song depending on the users liking which is of course very subjective. So we can analyze the rating dimensions in this regard and similar ways to explore dependencies of various natures between them. Those interpretations can motivate new kind of similarity measurements between users depending on different weightings of the rating dimensions.

There are different points of view to explore and research how the dimension weights may be interpreted and set. As proposed before the user should have the possibility to set them manually before every search and we will also provide predefined templates. Another way is to handle them class-dependent, so that all contents   (or the class it belongs to) will have a specific profile of dimension weights to boost its important rating dimensions and therefore the quality of the resulting similarity measurement. It is also possible that an object has more than one profile, depending on the searcher's perspective.

Maintaining user profiles - which is necessary for a collaborative filtering system - is always a privacy concern and must be done securely. Of course the user has to agree actively that a profile is created. In general the user may enter EUGAGER with and without identity verification which implies that at least two profiles are being used so that there is no way to find a connection between the anonymous and the official behaviour of the user.

The challenge posed by the proposed EUGAGER toolbox and applications goes beyond the state of the art. Thus research is necessary.

In order for the system to be useful in the e-government decision process, users´ opinions must be used to learn and create new knowledge. In the remaining part of this section, we will describe how we intend to perform these tasks.

Knowledge Creation. In order to create (synthesize) knowledge, we intend to build EUGAGER as a Darwinian system, meaning that we will design and implement algorithms that use and track human inputs to evolve new opinions and to evaluate existing ones (we will refer to these as "genetic algorithms" in the next pages. This process can be structured in several ways. We are currently considering two basic, alternative (but possibly complementary) structures: one in which users interaction is carried on sequential discrete rounds, and one in which the interaction is continuous over the time. Different aggregation criteria can be used for different approaches.

We now describe the procedure carried on discrete rounds. The process will proceed through rounds of subsequent generation of new opinions, and endorsement and evaluation of existing opinions. We shall define that an opinion A dominates an opinion B if all the users that have endorsed B have also endorsed A, plus some other users (see Figure 1). Note that in this regard we are not counting votes, but effectively considering which user has endorsed what, and confronting those sets of users opinions.

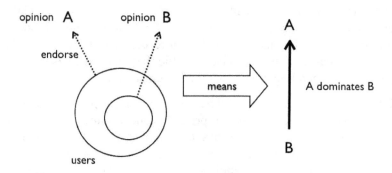

Figure 1 - Opinion A dominates opinion B

The procedure works as follows. We start by asking people to write their opinions in regard to a certain issue (Round 1.A). We then ask everybody which set of opinions they wish to endorse (Round 1.B). Once each user has cast her endorsement, we archive all the opinions dominated by other opinions, thus remaining with a Pareto front of opinions (i.e. a set of opinions where no opinion dominates another one, see Figure 2). We consider those opinions as the winning strategies of this round, say win. We then use the opinions in win to seed the next round. Next, we present win to the users as the set of surviving opinions, and we ask them to write new opinions, possibly trying to integrate—i.e. defining a new opinion dominating one or more old opinions—different existing opinions (Round 2.A). We then ask the users to endorse all the opinions they agree on (Round 2.B), compute the Pareto front of the result and assigning it to win (Round 2.C), and so on and so forth. Although the process seems to be well defined, there is a consistent research that needs to be done. For example, as defined here, the procedure only would end when the users have reached complete unanimity in their opinion. A different halting form needs to be defined. Also we need to test how successful such process is respect to real life issues.

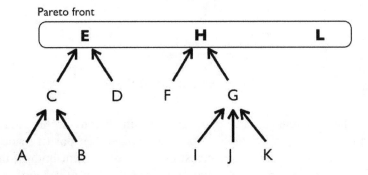

Figure 2 - Pareto front for a set of opinions

We now describe the procedure evolving on continuous time. A second possible process that we intend to investigate for the synthesis of group knowledge does not go through discrete time steps like the approach just described. Instead, in each instant all users can read the existing opinions, endorse the opinions that they agree on, and produce new opinions. Sometimes those opinions will be refinements of existing ones, in which case the new opinion will compete against its predecessor. Nonetheless, this would be a very unfair competition, as the new opinion will start later with fewer votes. In order to balance the unfairness of this situation, various possibilities can be tried and investigated. For example, we can sample the users endorsing the first proposal, if they endorse also the second one. Based on the result of this sampling we should be able to predict what would be the second opinion's relevance. We should then advertise the opinion based on the resulting relevance, thus helping to decrease the division between the potential endorsement that an opinion could have and its effective endorsement (see Figure 3). A wide variety of research needs to be carried out also in this context.

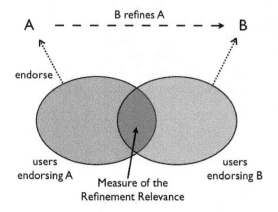

Figure 3 - Opinion Refinement Relevance

Both the discrete rounds procedure (with Pareto front) and the continuous time (with sampling) procedure have their positive side and their shortcomings. We shall investigate and implement both of them, analyse their differences, and then understand when is it better to use one or the other.

In every moment, users should be allowed to investigate the phylogenetic tree of opinions that they (or others) produced by a particular opinion, find out in each step why was an opinion favoured respect to another and how many people endorsed each. This data should be given both as raw data in a particular form (e.g. XML) and in a suitable graphical form. Raw data should permit any user to download, and reprocess the information, thus adding an extra layer of transparency.

Knowledge Learning. As opinions are collected, EUGAGER users will be allowed to search for them and archive them by adding to them new keywords (called tags). Thus each user will potentially be allowed to add her keywords to each opinion (even not hers). This is the base of what is called a broad folksonomy. Users will then be allowed to retrieve the opinions they have stored under a certain tag (or sets of tags). Using the (weighted) emergent set of tags, for each opinion we shall apply a measure that given every two opinions will find their nearest neighbours, thus letting users move from opinion to opinion.

We also shall implement a search box. To this aim in the following we explain how we should organize information. Users will be allowed to insert a set of keywords. Those words will be evaluated as a weighted set, their weights following a power law distribution and with steepness equivalent to the steepness of tags in a broad folksonomy. Using this information, the most relevant results will be returned. Since nearest neighbours opinions are linked to each other's, we can represent the set of opinions as a graph. This graph will not necessarily be connected. But each connected component (called cluster) will represent a set of opinions that can be reached moving through nearest neighbours, which could be a search option. Finally, we will present the set of clusters as a form of top down search. Note that this set of clusters will allow the user to look for broad areas of opinions. Moreover, clusters will give some feedback on the culture of the users having generated them, on which terms constitutes their ontologies and on which terms are considered related to each other.

1.1.3.2 Security

To achieve the objective described in 1.1.2, we will main focus on the following properties that will be considered as requirements for the design of the EUGAGER platform.

- *Authorization and Access Control.* The prevention of unauthorized use of a resource.
- *Authentication and Identity Management.* The provision of assurance of the claimed identity of an entity.
- *Availability.* The property of being accessible and usable upon demand.
- *Confidentiality.* The property that information is not made available or disclosed to unauthorized individuals, entities, or processes.
- *Integrity.* The property that information have not been altered or destroyed in an unauthorized manner.

A detailed threat analysis will be performed in the initial phase of the project, to identify the inherent risks of our architecture; through the identification of the possible threats and vulnerability of the architecture, we will identify the possible attacks to the system (such as, for example: password stealing, man in the middle attacks, identity spoofing, misuse, data modification or disclosure, privacy violation, etc). All the needed countermeasures will be implemented in order to minimize the residual risk.

For identity management and authentication, we should use a mechanism based on a two-factor authentication, such as the design of a distributed and software-based One-Time-Password Security mechanism to allow a usable but safe interaction of users with the EUGAGER platform. Authentication of users should be based on the primary identity associated by governments to a person's physical body, and the trustworthiness of a credential is usually determined by the strength of its links to this primary identity. Research in this field will focus on a suitable new protocol for user's authentication. This protocol should guarantee a high level of security (similar to the one achieved through the use of hardware tokens or smart cards), even preserving a high degree of usability, scalability, efficiency, and low costs. It's important to notice that the authentication API should allow all the tools to rely on a trusted authentication process performed by the EUGAGER toolbox, provided as a service to these tools.

At least two types of profile will be defined. One for non-verified users, e.g. users that will be able to access the tools, but that will not be allowed to take part in critical operations, such as the endorsement of proposals. The other profile will be defined for verified users, which will have a larger set of permissions (e.g. by using a one-time-password, they will be allowed to perform critical operations such as expressing their preference). While the first one could be a weak authentication, based for example on just a login-password mechanism, the second one has to be a strong authentication method, the one we will design in the research process. This twofold approach will allow a better participation to the entire process, as it will encourage users to subscribe our services though they don't want to fully identify themselves.

We will define the APIs to be used by the collaborative proposal tool and by all the other applications, which will be developed within this project (and later). The APIs will allow tools to perform only well-defined and restrictive operations on the data and structures inside the toolbox, to assure the trustworthiness of the platform and to avoid that a malicious application could perform dangerous operations.

As for Access Control, a RBAC (Role Based Access Control) [S:KMP02] [S:KMP05] methodology will be used to guarantee from misuse of the platform. Access Control Policies will be defined to achieve high security levels in the reference context. Also, constituency domains will be implemented using roles. The role configuration system will enable the precise definition of the set of users allowed to create constituency domains and to install and run applications on the platform.

Though we are not proposing an e-voting system, some of the requirements defined for e-voting systems are also valid in our environment and they need to be considered in our analysis. Research efforts will be dedicated to this objective, with the aim of designing the protocols to guarantee both confidentiality and integrity of the information, such as use of cryptography techniques (symmetric or asymmetric), SSL, MAC and Hashing. These techniques will be evaluated to define which of them we should integrate in our system and how, with the aim of creating a secure architecture as a whole.

Finally, we will formally verify the security of the whole system against the most of the well-known attacks. This is discussed in the following section.

Formal Verification for Security. We plan to use XACML to specify the control access rules that applications must adhere to in using toolbox APIs. Note however that manually designing proper control access rules with respect to given required properties is a difficult task. This is due mainly to the possibility that different users may collude to perform sequences of legitimate-if-taken-alone actions, in order to achieve forbidden goals. On the other hand, legitimate goals may be not achievable if the rules are too strict. Indeed, some works (e.g. [M:ZRG07]) have been devoted to a-priori verify via model checking if a given set of control access rules indeed allow legitimate goals and prevent malicious ones.

To this respect, we plan to address two different issues. First, we will apply model checking verification directly to XACML rules, to verify them with respect to given required properties. This will allow us to formally verify both that applications would not misuse our APIs, and that applications would indeed be able to achieve legitimate goals. While this resembles previous work, such as [M:ZRG07], to the best of our knowledge this is the first work to apply model checking techniques to e-government issues.

Second, we will work on the automatic synthesis of (XACML) control access rules, starting from the description of our APIs and the desired goals specifications. Note that this is different from the approach described in [M:ZRG07], where a given set of rules is verified to be sound, and then simply translated to XACML. On the other hand, automatic synthesis of control access rules may be rephrased as a supervisory control synthesis problem. In fact, control access rules may be seen as a way to forbid users actions to harm other users. Since a supervisor is software that restricts the behaviour of a system such that as much as possible of the given specifications are fulfilled, supervisory control theory [M:RW87] may be applied.

Resting on our experience on model checking based control and supervisory control design (e.g. see [M:Tro96, M:Tro97, M:Tro98, M:Tro99a, M:Tro99b, M:DIM+03, M:DIM+04, M:DIM+06, M:IMT07, M:MT07, M:PMT+08]) we will investigate methods and tools to synthesize control access rules.

1.1.3.3 Transparency

One of the major challenges for e-government frameworks is transparency. A system follows this property if the user can always be aware of government decisions and of other users opinions. The EUGAGER system will be formed by a set of trusted and untrusted components (see Sect. 1.1.4 for a global vision). The untrusted part of the system will be composed by applications. Thus we must supply the user with a method to understand the correctness of applications results.

In order to make EUGAGER satisfy transparency, inspired by Proof-Carrying Code technique [M:PCC97] we supply the user with an applications results checker (Tool Results Verifier). This tool will take as input an application result and will check—by using the toolbox API and directly inquiring raw data—on the correctness of such output. The method on which the checker will stand could be a formal specification of the application behaviour. This could be given in a specification language (e.g. CTL) or could be a trusted implementation—at the cost of waiting for results from the toolbox—of the application itself or other novel techniques. This methods entails a challenge for the transparency, thus research is necessary in this field.

1.1.3.4 Implementation Insights

Tool creators will use a tool manager to register their tool in first place and get an API key and provide the callback and index page URLs. Tools will get distribution on EUGAGER for the social actions users take within it. So, when a user performs a given social action (such as signing a petition, or posting a new proposal), it will generate a Feed Item on EUGAGER.

Tool creators can also use the EUGAGER API to get a user's name and profile picture and have that appear in their Tool (i.e.: Petition or Collaborative Proposals tool). This API will also support building and managing friend networks (perhaps using XFN [W:11] or FOAF [W:12]), status updates/microblogging, messaging and fine-grained Private Data Access Controls.

EUGAGER Tools will be able to make calls from the EUGAGER REST [W:13] API. Additional JavaScript methods (for example, to publish information back to EUGAGER from within a tool) as well as a special markup language to display selected data will be provided (so tools can, for example, request and display the list of friends for a particular user).

Figure 4 – EUGAGER Toolbox and applications Architecture

Tools can also implement their own API's. In particular, the Petition tool API will enable other tools to read, create or sign a petition, while allowing EUGAGER users to control how it can access and use their data (for example, user can choose not to allow the Petition Tool to microblog his petition signatures for a given constituency domain). This offers a rich environment where applications can talk to each other using the openness, transparency and security offered by EUGAGER while safeguarding user's right to Privacy. All these social features will be disabled by default, and users will have to explicitly activate them, becoming aware that they might be sharing sensible information about themselves.

1.1.4   Vision

We want to present a novel Governance and Participation Toolbox, aiming at satisfying most of the e-government needs. In this section we will provide a general vision on our proposed model, in particular stressing its architecture and functionalities.

1.1.4.1   Overall description

Components description. The system (see Figure 5) can be logically divided into *actors*, *toolbox*, *tools* (applications), *tools results checkers* and *authentication and tool manager*. In particular, the actors entail the *user*—e.g. the citizen, the governor, companies—and the system *administrator*. Toolbox, actors, results checkers and authentication and tool manager can be considered as *trusted* (the green boxes in the figure), while tools cannot (the red boxes).

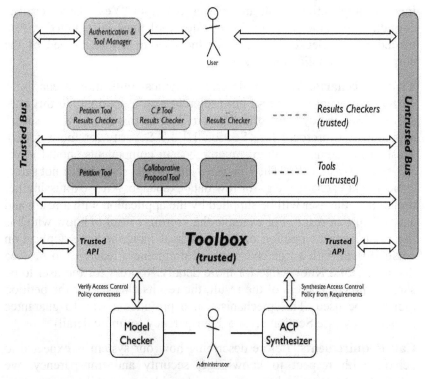

Figure 5 – System Architecture

On the trusted side, we are guaranteed since the core platform supplies the world with an interface composed by formally verified APIs. Moreover, actors and tools can access the platform via Access Control Policies (ACP). Such policies can be formally verified or—and this is one of our contributions—automatically synthesized. This is depicted in the bottom part of Figure 5. We provide the system with an ACP Model Checker, for the formal verification side, and with a tool for the Automatic Synthesis of an ACP, both usable by the Administrator. Users can access the system via an authenticated and secure channel (the left part of the figure), entailing all needed security properties, such as identification, confidentiality, integrity, etc (see Section 1.1.3.2). Moreover, users could log in the system simply using an anonymous profile, for operations not needing a high level of security.

On the other side, tools cannot be considered as trusted since they could behave in an intentionally malicious way, by giving the user wrong information. This motivates why we need trusted checkers, taking as input an application result and giving as output "Yes" if the result is correct, "No" otherwise. Each untrusted tool must be coupled with a trusted result checker in order for the user to be guaranteed of the correctness of applications results.

Typical scenario. We now describe a typical utilization scenario. A citizen may want to express her preference on a petition. To this aim, she accesses the system—the Petition Tool in this case—via a secure authentication protocol (see Section 1.1.4.3 Security for more detail). Most of the communications among system components should travel across the *Trusted Bus*. The *Untrusted Bus* is only thought for not safety critical data exchange, e.g. for raw data exchange. After expressing her preference, the user will be supplied by the application with a result and a proof for that result. For example the user may want to know which is the most frequent opinion on the matter at hand, and the application could answer with a tree endorsing all preferences received so far (see Section 1.1.4.2 Knowledge for more detail). In order for the user to be sure on the correctness of the result, the results checker for the petition tool can be used. This mechanism also provides a way to guarantee transparency (see Section 1.1.4.5 Transparency for more detail).

Call Requirements. Before describing how our system is expected to behave with respect to knowledge, security and transparency, we schematically describe how we intend to address the call requirements. This is done in the following Table.

Call Requirement	Addressed by:
Advanced tools embodying structural, organizational and new governance models	The tools that can run on top of EUGAGER, in particular, the innovation brought by the Collaborative Proposals Tool in terms of structural, organizational and new governance model.
To empower and engage all types of societal groups and communities	Anyone can quickly sign up, invite friends and use non-secure tools (engagement). Any verified user can participate in secure tools that are taken seriously by governments

Call Requirement	Addressed by:
	because of their proved data integrity, security and transparency (empowerment).
Enable them to utilize mass cooperation platforms	EUGAGER act as a "container" of tools for e-governance and e-participation, aggregating a unique and shared user-base in a social networking environment.
And allow governments to incorporate their input	Governments at any level can decide to create new or migrate existing tools to run on top of EUGAGER.
While safeguarding against misuse	EUGAGER offers primitives for security and data privacy for users and tools
These tools will enable the creation, learning, sharing and tracking of group knowledge Improved empowerment and engagement of individuals, groups and communities in policy making processes.	The Collaborative Proposals, Petitions and Polling tools provide ways to create, learn, share and track group knowledge by using the toolbox primitives. The Collaborative Proposals in particular empower citizens in the policy making process.
That cuts across language and cultural interpretation	The toolbox and its applications will be internationalized
They should also facilitate transparency and tracking of inputs to the policy making process Increased trust of the citizens through transparency and feedback of their contributions. More efficient collection of feedback to continuously improve governance.	The user-verifiability primitives allow users to check whether the tools are treating their data correctly and if the output of their contributed content is transparent (auditable).
The toolbox must include security	Granular privacy control access

Call Requirement	Addressed by:
identity and access controls to ensure privacy and, where appropriate, the delineation of constituency domains according to the specific needs of government applications	over user data and individual tools access rules. Tools make use of the constituency domain primitives to enable filtering and selecting relevant data for the user (i.e.: do not allow French users to sign Italian Petitions or do not allow Italian users to endorse German Proposals)
Improved prediction of impacts of policy measures, with increased contribution and involvement of individuals and communities, and based on intelligent and optimized use of vast public sector knowledge resources.	(Indirectly addressed) Will be possible when a government decides to launch an "official" tool within EUGAGER.
Strengthened competitive position of European industry in the fields of cooperation platforms, optimization, simulation and visualization tools	Creating a unified Citizen Engagement Platform to aggregate e-participation and e-governance tools managed directly by each EU member state governments gives a large competitive advantage in the mid-long term, when the user base is enlarged and offering of tools for several EU member states is reasonable (future calls could ask for specific tools to be built within EUGAGER)

1.1.4.2 Knowledge

The long-term vision would be to produce a system where different users (not just the policy makers, but also common citizens, and representatives of companies) would be able to ask for open questions. Those questions could be either addressed by any program user or only users that in a particular constituency domain (e.g. women, young men of age 18-35, Italian citizens, etc.). We can also suppose that only users inside certain policy domain will be allowed to endorse certain positions, but a different (potentially wider) user base can follow and seed the process with different opinions. This would allow more people to brainstorm the possible solutions for a problem, while safeguarding to the users involved the ability to effectively endorse certain positions. The users will then be allowed to produce an answer to a question, synthesize their opinion, and reach a partial agreement. This agreement will then be returned to the user that asked the question in the first place.

A broader vision would see users interacting with such a system at different levels. Policy makers will ask questions, and clarify what position do the citizen more broadly endorse. New positions will also be generated, by the conjugated effort of the citizens. And new solutions will then be proposed. Problems that affect the society will then have a tool to be effectively brainstormed through every person involved. And a solution found by a citizen will have a real chance to be endorsed through this process by a wide range of citizens, and potentially to be adopted as the policy of the whole nation, something that is nearly impossible up to now. Other users can also use this tool for different purposes: concerned groups of citizens will use it to integrate their efforts and positions to a single unanimous position.

Inside companies it could be used to start a wide brainstorm among the workers, as well as among the customers. Customers will be able to synthesize their opinions in a clear message that can be presented to a company. Generally the main change is that we would have a tool letting a group of people mediate their own position into a most endorsed position (a dialectic equivalent to the Maximum Common Denominator), and present that as their position.

1.1.4.3 Security

The described platform will ensure Security. In particular we will use several security techniques: secure authentication, digital signature, symmetric passwords for communications on HTTPS. All the techniques involved entail privacy, identification, integrity of data and confidentiality.

1.1.4.4 Transparency

The described platform will be Transparent. In other words, since the system users can trust tools results thus being able to transparently monitor for example petition results, citizens will be able to participate to government decisions.

1.2 Progress beyond the State of the Art

1.2.1 Knowledge Creation

The way in which we expect our tool to help people integrate their point of views is a novel approach for which very little if any research has been done. Its roots can be found in voting theory and game theory on the one side, and the study of genetic algorithms on the other.

The study of the ways in which a group of people can chose between competing strategies is as old as politics, and it heavily relies on mathematics. The field are game theory and voting theory (for a good review of the results, please refer to [K:TP08]).One of the basic presuppositions in such research is that the possible options are defined at the beginning. And once those are defined no late additions are then possible. In our tool we shall build a genetic algorithm of possible responses. Thus we shall produce and evaluate new possibilities, exploring in this way the space of possibilities.

Genetic algorithms use a combination of mutations and selection of the fittest to solve general, hard, problems. This technique is widely used in IT to solve complex problems. Yet when this technique is used the variations are generated in an automatic way. Then the result is evaluated usually using a fitness function (i.e. an algorithm) or sometimes by humans (see Dawkin ...). To produce a genetic algorithm of political options, automatically, we would need to be able to understand the semantic meaning of it. This result is a very hard, and for now unsolved, problem. We shall instead outsource both the creation of novelty and the evaluation of the results to human beings. In a decision making process it is quite common to have few people who are presenting the main alternatives, more people who are endorsing one or the other, and a very tiny minority which is trying to negotiate between the parts. What we will try to achieve is to expand the group of negotiator to become, potentially, to the whole group of people involved. Thus producing a human powered search engine of the possible solutions to a problem. A few explorative tests that have been done so far by non institutional websites, e.g. whitehouse2.org. In this website users are allowed to suggest what are the most urgent priorities that the president of the US should tackle. Interestingly they are also allowed to propose variations to existing priorities. The new priorities are then sent to the endorsers of the previous version, and if 70% of them endorse the new version, then the new version is substituted to the previous one. Although the experiment is very brave, and de facto successful, and academic analysis is needed on the various possible alternatives, and the results that would be generated with them. In passing we note that if 70% of the people who endorse priority A, would also endorse priority A', and if as a result priority A' was substituted to priority A', then some people are moved from a priority they were happy to endorse into another that they potentially might not endorse. Also if someone were to suggest back priority A, this would easily reach again the 100% of people endorsing it (since they were endorsing it in the first place), thus the system could be hacked to enter into a loop.

1.2.2 Formal Verification

Current state of the art.   To the best of our knowledge, model checking techniques have never been directly applied to e-government applications. Here, we will therefore deal with some works separately coping with the issues that are interesting in our project.

As for communications taking place between toolbox applications, toolboxes and users in our project, we will have to prove that the protocols we employ are indeed secure. To this aim, model checking techniques have been extensively used to verify given communication protocols, or to define frameworks to verify classes of communication protocols (see e.g. [M:MMS97], [M:MMS98], [M:ADMP01], [M:KKK08]).

Another important security issue is the one dealing with restricting user actions via a suitable control access policy mechanism. Some frameworks have been devised to both define and enforce a given set of control access rules, see e.g. XACML [M:XACML-web] and WS-Policies [M:WSP-web] enforced by jABC [M:HMHX07], [M:KMW08]. In [M:ZRG07] a method is presented to formally verify via model checking if a given control access rule specification indeed achieve given goals or prevent misuses, together with an automatic translation procedure of the given specification into XACML.

As for the automatic generation of policy access rules, the closest works are those on supervisory control theory [M:RW87]. We plan to apply model checking techniques for the generation of a supervisory controller. While this issue has been extensively investigated (see e.g. [M:ZS05]), to the best of our knowledge this is the first time such a technique is applied to e-government applications.

As for transparency, to the best of our knowledge there is not a method to automatically verify that an e-government application is indeed transparent, i.e. a technique providing the user with a formal proof that his endorsements have been correctly taken into account.

Shortcomings of current state of the art. To the best of our knowledge, model checking techniques have never been directly applied to e-government applications. This is indeed the major shortcoming of the current state of the art as for applying model checking to e-government applications.

Moreover, there are to the best of our knowledge no works dealing with transparency verification.

Finally, it is not possible to automatically synthesize a control access policy starting from an environment model and a goal specification.

Progress beyond the state of the art. In this project, we envisage to advance the current state of the art in model checking by applying model checking techniques to the verification of e-government applications.

First, we will apply already known model checking techniques to formally verify the security protocols we will employ in our project. This will result in the first application of model checking techniques to e-government applications.

Second, we will design a methodology to verify a given access control policy with respect to given specifications, in a way similar to [M:ZRG07].

Finally, we will design a methodology to formally synthesize a control access policy starting from an environment model and an error state specification. Note that this is not what is done in [M:ZRG07], where the control access policy is an input to the problem, and is simply syntactically translated into XACML once it has been verified.

1.2.3 Security

Current state of the art. The system we want to design has specific requirements in terms of confidentiality and integrity. As for the expression of the group knowledge, our system has to provide some form of voting. In this respect our system can be considered loosely related in its objective to an e-voting system. The requirements of e-voting systems have been thoroughly described in literature (see for example [S:VOL07], [S:CET08], [S:VOT04], [S:SAM06]), and it has been noticed that designing secure voting systems is extremely difficult since the requirements are apparently contradictory. When voting takes place in an electronic environment, the possibility of fraud is very high and ensuring the trust is not an easy task. People cannot easily trust the e-voting system unless they individually verify that their votes are cast, recorded and counted correctly. Individual verifiability is important to raise public trust in electronic voting.

The Election Markup Language (EML, [S:EML08]), the first XML specification of its kind, is a standard for the structured interchange of data among hardware, software, and service providers who engage in any aspect of providing election or voter services. Its function is to ensure open, secure, standardized and interoperable interfaces between the components of election systems. EML is a set of data and message definitions described as XML schemas.

One of the issues to focus on within the project is authentication of users and the identification management system.

Identity management refers to the process of representing and recognizing entities as digital identities in computer networks. Authentication, which is an integral part of identity management, serves to verify claims about holding specific identities. Identity management is therefore fundamental to, and sometimes include, other security constructs such as authorization and access control. Different identity management models will have different trust requirements. Since there are costs associated with establishing trust, it will be an advantage to have identity management models with simple trust requirements. [S:JOS05]

User authentication in computing systems traditionally depends on four factors: something you have (e.g., a hardware token), something you are (e.g., a fingerprint), something you know (e.g., a password), and where you are (for example inside or outside a company firewall, or proximity of login location to a personal GPS device).

The following are the most common methods of authentication:

Password – The password authentication method is the oldest and still most commonly used method for user authentication. However, password authentication is no longer considered adequately secure in many applications, because users can share their passwords and because replay attacks have become common.

One-Time-Password – The one-time-password, or OTP, authentication method can be divided into two sub-types. Time-based methods rely on the transformation of a shared secret and a time value that is synchronized between the server and the client. Event-based methods rely on the transformation of a shared secret and an event count that is synchronized between the server and the client.

Challenge / Response – Is usually based on a shared-secret transformation using symmetric-key hashing techniques. The server side sends the client a challenge, and the client uses this challenge and the shared secret as input to the transformation. The resulting output is the response, which is then sent to the server.

Transaction Signing – This method is a more advanced version of challenge / response, where the user confirms certain details of the transaction. These details are then input into the algorithmic computation, often based on symmetric cryptography. Usually the server would transmit the specific details and the user would type them into a token or an unconnected smart card reader. The token / reader would then display a response that is sent to the server for verification.

User certificate – Certificate-based authentication uses public-key encryption techniques, supported by a public-key infrastructure (PKI) for key and certificate management. Digital certificates are issued by a certification authority and they bind the user's identity to their public key. In a typical certificate-based authentication protocol, the client uses its private key to sign a challenge from the server, and the server verifies the signature using the client's certificate.

Biometric - Biometric authentication methods are based on a physiological characteristic of a user, such as a fingerprint, iris image or facial image. Biometric authentication represents the "what you are" component of multi-factor authentication. Biometric authentication is based on data-matching of the captured biometric characteristic to a stored template.

Device fingerprint – A Web application may examine a persistent cookie, the source IP address and the type and version of the remote user agent. This information can be used to identify suspected impersonation attacks. However, because users legitimately change or update their browsers periodically, this technique is subject to "false positives". Nevertheless, it can be used as one in a set of risk metrics to decide when step-up authentication is required.

Device certificate – Certificates can be embedded in a variety of network devices, such as cable modems, set-top boxes and WiMax-compliant subscriber stations.

Trusted platform module – Trusted platform modules can be used to strongly authenticate appropriately equipped computing devices.

Passwords remain the most common mechanism for user authentication in computer-security systems. Their various drawbacks, like poor selection by users and vulnerability to capture, are prompting a rapidly mounting adoption of hardware authentication tokens. A workable authentication system requires at least two modes of authentication [S:BJR06]. For example, consumers' mobile phones offer a platform for authentication that is increasingly favoured by financial institutions for high-risk online transactions (but less often for password recovery). Mobile-phone based authentication can operate in several ways, for example an institution can transmit an authentication code to a phone via SMS messaging, and request that the user enter the code into a web form.

Some frameworks have been designed for single-sign-on and federated authentication:

Shibboleth [S:SHI09] is an initiative of Internet 2 – a consortium of universities that is developing new internet technologies. Shibboleth uses SAML (Security Assertion Markup Language) as set of rules on how information about identity should be exchanged and authenticated. Shibboleth provides for federated authentication (a certificate issued by one university can be accepted by another university) and has built-in privacy controls that allow users to decide how much information to share.

Kerberos [S:KER94] is another authentication protocol and was one of the first network authentication technologies to be developed. It is widely used. Kerberos uses a "key distribution centre" – KDC – as a trusted third party who issues encrypted identifying "tickets" to users. The users can then use the tickets to authentications each other's assertion of identity. One of the attractions of Kerberos is that it allows for "single sign on," which means that once a ticket has been issued by the KDC it can be used more than once and on different networks. Kerberos pre-dates Web 2.0 but it has been adopted for use by many of the new web services.

OpenID [S:OPID09] also provides for single sign-on. An OpenID user registers with an "Identity Provider." Once they are registered, the user makes an assertion of identity to a site using OpenID by providing an Internet address to links back to the Open ID provider. This secure link confirms the identity assertion. Once an OpenID account is created with one identity provider, it can be used with any other website using OpenID.

Higgins is an open source project that began in 2003 that is supported by IBM and Novell. Higgins is intended to allow users to decide what information to share in different contexts (e.g. people share health information with a doctor, but not with a job search site) and uses. Higgins uses a framework that allows information from multiple sources to be shared in carefully controlled ways based on the underlying relationships. Higgins does not itself authenticate identity, but let's programmers write "plug-in" applications that can work with multiple, different authentication technologies.

CardSpace is a Microsoft identity management system similar in process to Higgins. CardSpace allows a user to create digital identity cards, each of which contains a different amount of information about themselves. The user can then decide which card to use when they authenticate themselves with a website. CardSpace allows users to create an identity document for themselves and decide what information it should contain, or, for more valuable transactions, get an identity document issued by a trusted identity provider, such as a bank or other commercial service or governmental agency.

Liberty Alliance is a standards-setting body for authentication technologies. Liberty has developed technical standards that allow different authentication technologies to interoperate. Liberty's Identity Assurance Framework (IAF) outlines policies and business rules against which identity services can be assessed for trust. Liberty has begun work on an Identity Governance Framework (IGF) that will use "trust frameworks" - rules on how a credential should be issued, verified and managed – to determine how much a credential can be trusted.

OAuth [S:OAUTH06] protocol enables websites or applications (Consumers) to access Protected Resources from a web service (Service Provider) via an API, without requiring Users to disclose their Service Provider credentials to the Consumers. More generally, OAuth creates a freely-implementable and generic methodology for API authentication.

There are substantial differences among these technologies and architectures and they are in some ways competitors. None has universal acceptance. The common pattern with these technologies is that they offer greater precision and control in the use of personal data and greater acceptance of heterogeneity and the need for interoperability. Authentication protocols, like Higgins, OpenID and CardSpace, also extend the ability of users to control the release of their personal information as part of the authentication process. These new approaches to authentication provide the technological basis for progress, but they face the same set of policy related problems that hampered PKI and the earlier generations of authentication technologies.

Access control techniques are sometimes categorized as either discretionary or non-discretionary. The three most widely recognized models are Discretionary Access Control (DAC), Mandatory Access Control (MAC), and Role Based Access Control (RBAC). MAC and RBAC are both non-discretionary.

Role based access control [S:KMP02] [S:KMP05] allows policies to be specified in terms of subject roles rather than strictly in terms of individual subject identities. This is important for scalability and manageability of access control systems.

The policies can answer three types of questions:

1. If a subject has roles R1 , R2, ... Rn enabled, can subject X access a given resource using a given action?

2. Is subject X allowed to have role Ri enabled?

3. If a subject has roles R1 , R2, ... Rn enabled, does that mean the subject will have permissions associated with a given role R'? That is, is role R' either equal to or junior to any of roles R1 , R2, ...Rn?

In some cases, role attributes might come from an identity management service that maintains information about a user, including the subject's assigned or allowed roles; the identity management service acts as the Role Enablement Authority. This service might store static role attributes in an LDAP directory.

Role based access control in a web environment can be realized through the XACML [S:XACML05] language. XACML, eXtensible Access Control Markup Language, is an XML based standard language for defining access control policies. XACML is based on attributes of subjects, resources, actions and the environment, which are used to describe an access request. The complete set of attributes used in the processing of a request is known as the request context. The policy language specifies the access control requirements that a request must demonstrate in order for a user to be granted access. XACML policies are functional expressions that pull their input from the request context [S:MAZ04]. When a request context is evaluated against a set of policies, a response is calculated as specified by the semantics of the policy format and the processing model. The response can either be Permit, Deny, NotApplicable or Indeterminate. The trusted policies need no special validation and form the roots of trust (analogous to the self signed certificates of root CAs in PKI). The policies with untrusted issuers have to be validated against the trusted policies. The validation process is called reduction and is performed when an access request is evaluated.

Shortcomings of current state of the art. This platform, as we have described in the previous paragraphs, has specific requirements in terms of confidentiality and integrity. As for the expression of the group knowledge, our system should provide some form of voting. Designing secure voting systems is extremely difficult since the requirements are apparently contradictory. In the literature, there is no protocol which satisfies receipt-freeness, uncoercibility and individual verifiability at the same time, even with conditions or assumptions [S:SAM06]. As for authentication, the existent protocols have revealed too weak (it is easy for an attacker to spoof its identity) or, when considered safe, sometimes too expensive to deploy (such as the use of smart card and PKIs). Furthermore, a common approach is to add security mechanisms to an already existent software architecture. The experience/statistics show that the latter approach results in weaker system, and so the security mechanisms can be often bypassed.

Progress beyond the state of the art. Research on authentication mechanisms will focus on a suitable new mechanism for user's authentication. This protocol should guarantee a high level of security (similar to the one achieved through the use of hardware tokens or smart cards), even preserving a high degree of usability, scalability, efficiency, and low costs. Another important research issue is to find a trade off among the different e-voting requirements proposed in the literature. Such trade-off should allow the design and implementation of an efficient and secure system to support the creation, learning, sharing and tracking of group knowledge in an e-government environment.

1.2.4   Web 2.0

Current state of the art. The term "Web2.0" is now well-know all over the Internet [W:web2-web]. More recently, "Government2.0" has gained a lot of traction. The world is watching closely as the United States' President Barack Obama pushes for greater citizen involvement in the government after making large use of social networks and social media tools like Twitter and YouTube in his presidential campaign[W:wired-web].

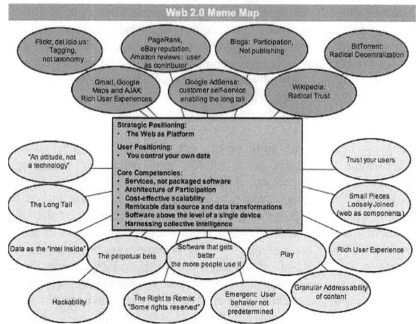

Figure 6 – Web 2.0 Meme Map (*Source: O'Reilly Media [W:web2-web]*)

Active developers from many Free/Libre Open Source (FLOSS) communities keep launching independent e-participation tools trying to dialogue with their political representatives [W:wh-web][W:dec-web], or even to bypass them [W:metagov-web][W:tgde-web].

Some Governments also launched their own initiatives. Some with huge success (the official White House "Open for Questions" page counts 92,905 people, 104,085 questions and 3,607,901 casted votes in just a few days online [W:wh-q-web]); others with less...[W:cnipa-web]

Web 2.0 applications are built of a network of cooperating data services. The EUGAGER platform aims to offer web services interfaces and content syndication, and re-use the data services of others through the iteration between EUGAGER Tools, by supporting a lightweight programming model that allow for loosely-coupled systems.

Web 2.0 is harnessing collective intelligence, turning the web into a kind of global brain (resulting in the so-called "Wisdom of Crowds") [W:SJ05]. Facebook, MySpace, LinkedIn and many others are doing their part for friendship relations, entertainment and business. Why can't Europe take advantage of this momentum to create the largest Citizen Engagement Platform for e-participation and e-government?

Tags. One of our basic tools will be a broad folksonomy, which we shall use to organise, cluster, search, and retrieve information. Broad folksonomy are meta-data generated by a community of users when they are all allowed to "tag" (apply various keywords) to different resources, for their own personal use. Tags have been shown to follow a Power Law distribution [K:C07]. It has also been shown that the tags used for a single resource define a metric [K:C08] between the resources. We aim to use this metric to cluster the generated input from the users, and to provide, given an input, the nearest neighbours. Thus permitting to travel the space of resources horizontally. As resources tend to be tagged following a power law, this produces many resources that are generally simply unavailable. And hard to find through a direct search. Note that there have been some works in using folksonomies to search for information [K:M08], with mixed results. Those research focused on using tagclouds (a visual delivery of the information produced by tag clouds) ([K:SC08], [K:S08], [K:B08], [K:KL07]) to let pick the keywords they wanted to search. So the procedure was still a topdown search. By employing a "nearest neighbours" type of search we aim to let people reach every resource, through a series of refinement in their search. At each level of refinement finding better resources. This will be possible only through resources that are connected. For this reason we aim to provide a top down vision of the clusters of information that has been generated. Although there have been in the past examples of clustering of the information provided through tags [K:M05], we aim to utilise the novel information that has so far been produced to generate more precise clusters. On passing we note that the tags that people uses are representatives of their culture. As such we expect the emerging clusters to be equally representatives. No work that we are aware of has been done to study how different cultures organise through tags differently.

Shortcomings of current state of the art. Current e-participation and e-governance sites have a difficult time reaching critical-mass and enlarging their user base like recent Web2.0 and social sites are able to do in just a few months. In the few cases they succeeded the output cannot be considered "statistically relevant" because there wasn't a true validation of the user's identity (i.e.: avoiding the same person creating multiple accounts; avoiding the participation from people in non-relevant geographical areas), and therefore Governments listen but are not sure whether to take these user inputs seriously enough.

Also, the current offering of e-participation tools (released officially by governments or created by independent citizens) are very fragmented, and there isn't a central place to find them and interact with other people with similar interests.

The Facebook Platform/Facebook Connect [W:fb-web][W:fbc-web] and Google's Open Social/Google Friend Connect [W:opensoc-web][W:fc-web] try to make this less of an issue, but Governments cannot be dependent of proprietary technology and cannot directly participate in the development and roadmap of such platforms to introduce the security, transparency and privacy requirements they need to run secure tools and get "statistically relevant" outputs, even more when they compete directly with each other [W:techcr-web].

Progress beyond the state of the art. EUGAGER aims to be the largest ecosystem of e-participation and e-governance applications, released (or migrated) officially by governments at all levels, independent users or by Open Source communities. Internationalization and definition of constituency domains will provide a new approach to manage how citizens will relate with these tools, by enabling a multi-cultural knowledge interchange and harnessing the collective intelligence for the benefit of the citizens themselves.

Facebook, MySpace, Hi5, Orkut, LinkedIn and several well-known social networking sites offer today the possibility of running internal widgets or applications, or connect with external sites (Facebook Connect, Google Friend Connect), but still they are unsuited for governmental use and to build a network around citizen empowerment and engagement. Actual initiatives launched by each EU Member State are unconnected, do not share their user base or their data, do not expose open API's to serve public data or to interface with others.

EUGAGER will advance all of these issues in its core platform, while considering the privacy, security and transparency issues that concern today most users of social networking sites.

1.2.5 Information Filtering

Current state of the art. The main task of information filtering is the classification of documents in a dynamic collection. Typical fields of application are newsgroups [B:RIS+94], where new contributions are sorted by relevance for the active user, or spam filters in email applications. The approaches can be further classified in content based [B:MGT+87] and collaborative ones and mixed forms of both. Collaborative information filtering uses the community knowledge to solve the classification problem to assist users and that is what EUGAGER is also going to do.

Recommender systems [B:RV97, B:PP04] define a subclass of collaborative information filtering systems concentrating on the recommendation of items to users. Those items can be actual items in a web-shop but can also be abstract things such as taste of music. Most recommendation algorithms either use a model - which they create based on user behaviour - or a memory based approach which maintains user profiles to compute personalized recommendations. The information needed for a profile can be actively generated by the community, e.g. by rating items, or can be collected passively by observing the user's behaviour such as watching an description of an item or listening to a song. The next step is the computation of similarities between users with the goal of finding similar users whose opinions may help each other like they would in real social life. Similarity measures map the profiles of two users to a degree of similarity. Typical measures are the Pearson correlation coefficient [B:RIS94] and the Cosine measure, which is also commonly used in text retrieval (more precise: in the vector space model [B:S71]).

Often, profiles are collections of one-dimensional ratings of items by users (e.g. one to five stars) implying that the items are comparable on the given scale. This leads automatically to the problem of comparing apples with oranges if the collection contains inhomogeneous items [B:AT05]. Also the rating of an item often depends on additional contextual information which leads to multidimensional recommendation models [B:AK07]. Having more than one rating dimension or criteria makes the usage of multiple similarity measures possible. To achieve that, different weighting schemes of the dimensions can be used. The user may now choose the weights which lead to the best recommendation (depending on the item class context). This principle of a meta recommender [B:SK02] promises customisable personalised results if the user has the expertise and patience to adjust the weights. If not, he may always fall back to preset weighting templates or to the standard one dimensional rating.

Shortcomings of current state of the art. The research in the field of multidimensional recommender systems is not very broad and a new case study in the context of EUGAGER would be very helpful. Especially evaluations of multidimensional approaches on different item domains are needed. Also, to the best of our knowledge, there have been no attempts to automatically adjust or generate multidimensional similarity measures by using a collaborative approach to explore domain dependencies. The design of a useful interface, which has to be understood and accepted by the user, is another shortcoming in current multidimensional recommender systems.

Progress beyond the state of the art. Because the benefit of a meta recommender system depends on the will of the user to choose the appropriate weightings - which is likely interpreted as unloved work or simply out of the users´ scope - it is a reasonable effort to help him doing this in some way. Assuming that it is not uncommon that the optimal weighting scheme is somehow dependent on the type of item or object the user wants a recommendation for, the idea would now be to (again) use the community knowledge to create weighting schemes for those classes of items, thus abstracting from predefined classes. EUGAGER´s community would provide an ideal setting to research, implement and evaluate new approaches in this direction. Further the anticipated improvement in recommendation quality would simultaneously lead to more comfort hopefully again leading to more involvement of the European users in EUGAGER´s aim of e-governance and e-participation.

1.3 S/T Methodology and Associated Work Plan

1.3.1 Overall Strategy of the Work Plan

The strategy of the project is to pursue in parallel research, implementation, dissemination and exploitation activities in order to achieve project objectives.

Figure 7 schematically represents the study logic.

The heart of the project is Toolbox Platform Design: platform requirements analysis include knowledge, security and transparency issues. This will stimulate research in such areas to analyse existing technologies and developing new approaches to face the severe problems posed by e-government applications. Conversely, security, knowledge and transparency aspects will influence platform design from the beginning. Moreover, research in these areas are interconnected, and several trade-offs may arise: for example between transparency and security.

The platform will provide trusted APIs with certified security properties. Prototype and Demonstration activity concerns the implementation of three tools to demonstrate toolbox functionality. The software will be released as open source, actively maintained, and tested on meaningful case studies.

During the development of EUGAGER, the Dissemination activities will incrementally make available the results (free software, science advancements) provided by the definition of exploitation scenario and by the implementation of services: these will be achieved through website, workshops, publications and online campaigns oriented to the scientific communities, open source communities, and EU citizens.

As for Exploitation, governments at all levels will be approached to choose EUGAGER as the base platform for their next e-participation and e-governance tools. As a project result, a framework for the development of on-line services for e-government will be presented. In order to demonstrate the capabilities of our framework, we will implement some applications using the API interface with the platform and giving to the user provable results.

In the long term, we expect to approach businesses interested in learning how to develop or integrate software for the EUGAGER platform, as they can offer services for governments in their home countries, stimulating also local software industry. We will thus exploit the opportunity to offer training sessions to the private companies that are interested in offering such kinds of services.

Finally, we will exploit our network of contacts with current and active FLOSS Communities running independent e-participation initiatives and invite them to early adopt EUGAGER as a base platform, to join forces in reaching a critical-mass and eventually transforming it into a one-stop-shop for citizen engagement tools.

Risk assessment. No specific risk is envisaged that could seriously affect or limit the implementation of the project, as explained below.

The experience ensures that all basic knowledge about the domains (web platforms, knowledge, security and transparency) is available. The relevant improvement pursued by EUGAGER relies mainly on the comparison and integration of such knowledge in an e-government environment, and no relevant risk can be identified in this context.

Concerning development activities, possible risks could be related to the use of open source software, as limited or none maintenance and scarce documentation; of course, the selection of software will minimise such shortcomings; in the case they would occur, they would create a delay in the platform implementation; however, the time schedule of the project has been defined also taking into account such eventual delays.

1.3.2 Project Schedule

The duration of the project is three years.

Figure 7 illustrates how work packages and their main components will iterate and shows their interdependencies.

Figure 8 shows the Gantt diagram of the project, where the duration of each work package (also shown in Table 1.3-a) is illustrated.

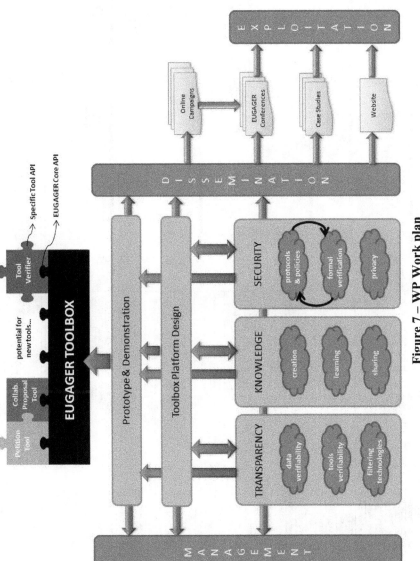

Figure 7 – WP Work plan

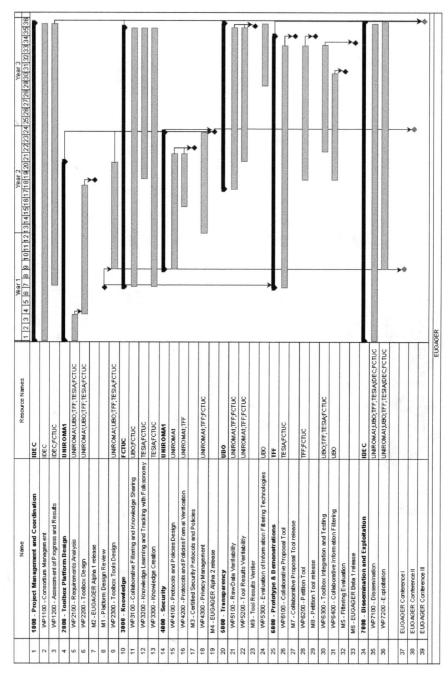

Figure 8 – GANTT chart for EUGAGER

1.3.3 Detailed Work Description

Table 1.3-a - Work package list

Work package No[1]	Work package title	Type of act.[2]	Lead partic no.[3]	Person mos[4]	Strt M[5]	End M[5]
WP1000	Project Management and Coordination	MGT	1 IDEC	1	1	36
WP1100	Consortium Management	MGT	1 IDEC	4	1	36
WP1200	Assessment of Progress and Results	MGT	1 IDEC	6	7	36
WP2000	Toolbox Platform Design	RTD	2 UNIROMA1	1	1	20
WP2100	Requirements Analysis	RTD	2 UNIROMA1	9	1	3
WP2200	Toolbox Design	RTD	2 UNIROMA1	33	4	17
WP2300	Toolbox Tools Design	RTD	3 TFF	18	9	20
WP3000	Knowledge	RTD	4 FCTUC	1	7	35
WP3100	Collaborative Filtering and Knowledge Sharing	RTD	6 UBO	33	7	35
WP3200	Knowledge Learning and Tracking with Folksonomy	RTD	4 FCTUC	22,5	19	35
WP3300	Knowledge Creation	RTD	4 FCTUC	31	7	35
WP4000	Security	RTD	2 UNIROMA1	1	9	24
WP4100	Protocols and Policies Design	RTD	2 UNIROMA1	16	9	21
WP4200	Protocols and Policies Formal Verification	RTD	2 UNIROMA1	11,75	16	21

[1] Workpackage number: WP 1 – WP n.
[2] RTD = Research and technological development; DEM = Demonstration; MGT = Management of the consortium
[3] Number of the participant leading the work in this Work Package.
[4] The total number of person-months allocated to each work package.
[5] Measured in months from the project start date (month 1).

WP4300	Privacy Management	RTD	2 UNIROMA1	12,75	13	24
WP5000	Transparency	RTD	6 UBO	1	18	36
WP5100	Raw Data Verifiability	RTD	2 UNIROMA1	9,5	18	35
WP5200	Tool Results Verifiability	RTD	2 UNIROMA1	9,5	21	35
WP5300	Evaluation of Information Filtering Technologies	RTD	6 UBO	6	29	36
WP6000	Prototype & Demonstrations	DEM	3 TFF	1	6	34
WP6100	Collaborative Proposal Tool	DEM	5 TESIA	30,5	6	33
WP6200	Petition Tool	DEM	3 TFF	10,5	19	33
WP6300	Toolbox Integration and Testing	DEM	5 TESIA	13,7	22	33
WP6400	Collaborative Information Filtering	DEM	6 UBO	3,5	19	30
WP7000	Dissemination and Exploitation	MGT	1 IDEC	1	1	36
WP7100	Dissemination	MGT	1 IDEC	15,5	1	36
WP7200	Exploitation	MGT	4 FCTUC	15,5	9	36
	TOTAL			318,2		

Table 1.3-b - List of Deliverables

Del. no. [6]	Deliverable name	WP no.	Nature [7]	Dissemi -nation [8]	Delivery date [9] (proj. month)
D1001	Periodic Activity Report	1	R	CO	6, 12, 18, 24, 30, 36
D1002	Updated Implementation Plan	1	R	RE	1, 12, 24,36
D1101	Financial Plan	1	R	CO	1
D1102	Management Report	1	R	CO	6, 12, 18, 24, 30, 36
D1103	Communication Platform	1	O	CO	1
D1201	Documentation Management Report	1	R	CO	1
D2011	Coordination document	2	R	CO	1, 12
D2141	Requirements Description	2	R	PU	3
D2211	Toolbox Platform Architecture Documentation	2	R	PU	4
D2221	EUGAGER API definition	2	R	PU	10
D2231	EUGAGER Core Database Model	2	P	PU	9

---

[6]   Deliverable numbers in order of delivery dates.
[7]   Nature of the deliverable: **R** = Report, **P** = Prototype, **D** = Demonstrator, **O** = Other
[8]   Dissemination level: **PU** = Public, **PP** = Restricted to other programme participants (including the Commission Services), **RE** = Restricted to a group specified by the consortium (including the Commission Services), **CO** = Confidential, only for members of the consortium (including the Commission Services).
[9]   Measured in months from the project start date (month 1).

Del. no.[6]	Deliverable name	WP no.	Nature[7]	Dissemi -nation[8]	Delivery date[9] (proj. month)
D2232	EUGAGER API v1	2	P	PU	11
D2241	EUGAGER API v2	2	P	PU	14
D2261	EUGAGER Core Platform Prototype	2	P	PU	17
D2311	Authentication and Tool Manager Architecture Documentation	2	R	PU	16
D2341	Authentication and Tool Manager Prototype	2	P	PU	20
D2351	User Profile and Preferences Page	2	P	PU	18
D2352	User Activity Stream Page	2	P	PU	20
D3011	Coordination Document	3	R	CO	7, 19
D3111	Results of the R&D of a multidimensional rating system for user content	3	R	PU	33
D3121	Analysis of rating-dimensions and object-dependencies (results)	3	R	PU	18
D3131	Description of similarity measures based on users´ tags	3	R	PU	33
D3141	Description of similarity measures on multidimensional ratings	3	R	PU	33
D3151	Trust Algorithm Description	3	R	PU	33
D3161	Statistical Analysis	3	R	PU	35

Del. no. [6]	Deliverable name	WP no.	Nature[7]	Dissemi -nation[8]	Delivery date[9] (proj. month)
	Results				
D3211	Graph Generation Algorithm Description and Analysis of Performance	3	R	PU	21
D3221	Search Algorithm Description and Analysis of Performance	3	R	PU	24
D3231	Emergent Clusters Analysis and Analysis of Performance	3	R	PU	27
D3241	Similarity Measures Description	3	R	PU	35
D3251	Communities Clusters Comparison Report	3	R	PU	32
D3252	Extracted Information Analysis	3	R	PU	35
D3311	Pareto Front Genetic Algorithm Description	3	R	PU	12
D3312	Pareto Front Results Description	3	R	PU	24
D3321	Continuous Genetic Algorithms Description	3	R	PU	18
D3322	Continuous Genetic Algorithms Results	3	R	PU	30
D4011	Coordination Document	4	R	CO	9;18
D4111	Authentication Protocol Description	4	R	PU	16

Del. no. [6]	Deliverable name	WP no.	Nature[7]	Dissemi -nation[8]	Delivery date[9] (proj. month)
D4121	Access Control Policies Description	4	R	PU	16
D4141	Integrity and Confidentiality Report	4	R	PU	21
D4211	Authentication Protocol Verification Description	4	R	PU	18
D4221	Access Control Policies Verification Description	4	R	PU	18
D4222	Access Control Policies Verification Tool	4	P	PU	21
D4231	Access Control Policies Automatic Synthesis Description	4	R	PU	19
D4232	Access Control Policies Automatic Synthesis Tool	4	P	PU	21
D4241	Web Application Security Analysis Results	4	R	PU	17
D4311	Requirements Analysis for Toolbox User Privacy Management Description	4	R	PU	16
D4321	Architecture Definition for Toolbox User Privacy Management	4	R	PU	19

Del. no. [6]	Deliverable name	WP no.	Nature[7]	Dissemi -nation[8]	Delivery date[9] (proj. month)
	Documentation				
D4331	Tools Supporting Granular User Privacy Controls	4	P	PU	24
D4341	Requirements Analysis for Tools Private Data Access Controls Definition	4	R	PU	16
D4351	Architecture for Tools Private Data Access Controls Documentation	4	R	PU	19
D4361	Implementation of Tools Private Data Access Controls	4	P	PU	24
D5011	Coordination Document	5	R	CO	21, 28
D5111	Requirements Analysis Description	5	R	PU	19
D5121	Methodology Design Description	5	R	PU	28
D5131	Tool for Raw Data Verifiability	5	P	PU	35
D5211	Requirements Analysis Description	5	R	PU	22
D5221	Methodology Design Description	5	R	PU	30
D5231	Tool for Application Results Verifiability	5	P	PU	35
D5311	Test collection from processed user profiles	5	O	RE	34

Del. no.[6]	Deliverable name	WP no.	Nature[7]	Dissemi -nation[8]	Delivery date[9] (proj. month)
D5321	Description of Evaluation procedure	5	R	PU	32
D5331	Implementation and results	5	P	PU	36
D6011	Coordination Document	6	R	CO	6, 18, 26
D6111	Collaborative Proposal Tool Documentation	6	R	PU	32
D6171	Collaborative Proposal Tool Standalone Test Case	6	D	PU	9
D6172	Collaborative Proposal Tool Release v1	6	P	PU	18
D6173	Collaborative Proposal Tool API	6	P	PU	27
D6174	Collaborative Proposal Tool Release v2	6	P	PU	33
D6211	Petition Tool Documentation	6	R	PU	20
D6241	Petition Tool API	6	P	PU	24
D6251	Petition Tool Release	6	P	PU	34
D6311	Trusted API Testing Report	6	R	PU	30
D6321	Privacy Management Testing Report	6	R	PU	28
D6331	Tools Privacy Management Integration Report	6	R	PU	31
D6341	Platform Testing Report	6	R	PU	32
D6411	Requirements	6	R	PU	30

Del. no. [6]	Deliverable name	WP no.	Nature[7]	Dissemi -nation[8]	Delivery date[9] (proj. month)
	Description				
D6421	Architecture Documentation	6	R	PU	30
D6431	Implementation Documentation	6	P	PU	30
D7011	Dissemination Plan	7	R	CO	1, 12, 24
D7111	EUGAGER Logo and color palette	7	O	PU	2
D7121	Project Website and Development Mailing List	7	O	PU	2
D7122	Project SVN and Bug Tracking System	7	O	RE	6
D7131	Online Campaign - Round 1	7	R	CO	9
D7132	Online Campaign - Round 2	7	R	CO	24
D7133	Online Campaign - Round 3	7	R	CO	36
D7141	I EUGAGER Conference	7	O	PU	9
D7142	II EUGAGER Conference	7	O	PU	24
D7143	III EUGAGER Conference	7	O	PU	36
D7151	Universities Case Study	7	R	PU	36
D7161	Government Case Study	7	R	PU	36
D7171	FLOSS Communities Case Study	7	R	PU	36
D7231	Exploitation Plan	7	R	RE	18
D7232	Exploitation Report	7	R	RE	36

Table 1.3-c - List of Milestones

Mil.	Milestone name	WP(s) involved	Date	Means of verification
M1	Platform Design Review	WP2	7	Documentation ready for implementation step and published on the project website
M2	EUGAGER Alpha 1 release	WP2, WP6, WP7	19	Prototype running, code released on SVN and validated by a user group
M3	Certified Security Protocols and Policies	WP2, WP4, WP7	22	Report on Security Protocols and Policies specification and formal verification via model checking ready and published on the project website
M4	EUGAGER Alpha 2 release	WP2, WP3, WP4, WP6, WP7	24	Prototype running, code released on SVN and validated by a user group
M5	Filtering Evaluation	WP3, WP5, WP7	31	Report on Filtering Technologies ready and published on the project website
M6	EUGAGER Beta 1 release	WP3, WP4, WP5, WP6, WP7	34	Prototype running, code released on SVN and validated by a user group
M7	Collaborative Proposal Tool release	WP3, WP5, WP6, WP7	34	Prototype running, code released on SVN and validated by a user group
M8	Petition Tool release	WP6, WP7	34	Prototype running, code released on SVN and validated by a user group
M9	Tool Results Verifier	WP5, WP7	36	Prototype running, code released on SVN and validated by a user group

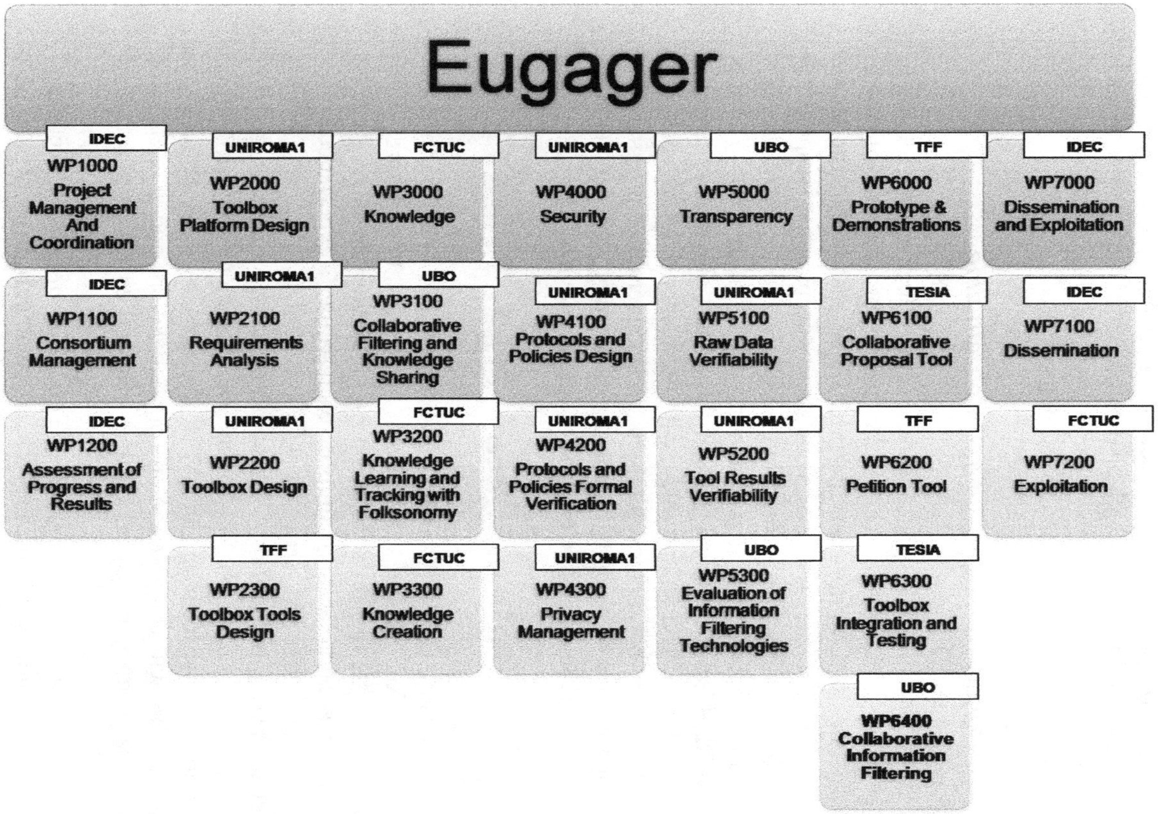

Figure 9 – EUGAGER Work Breakdown

Detailed List of Work Packages

The activities of EUGAGER project are grouped in Work Packages (WP) as shown in Figure 9 (which also includes the short names of each WP leader).
Each WP is briefly described in the following.

WP1000: Project Management and Coordination
WP Responsible: IDEC
Main aims of the workpackage are the effective coordination, administration and monitoring of the whole programme of work, especially for the Commission interface. That means that the whole consortium under the leadership of the workpackage responsible ensures not only the coordination but also the report project progress and status to Commission. It is also very important to identify events which could affect the achievement of the project objectives, and plan recovery actions. The coordinator will be responsible for ensuring project runs smoothly, achieves targets and deliverables, provides full project activity and financial reports to Commission to required deadlines, payments are made on time to consortium partners.

WP1100: Consortium Management
WP Responsible: IDEC
In order to ensure the full cooperation-participation of all partners, an extensive division of tasks has been performed that assures their involvement in the project's tasks. Special attention has been given so that task allocation is fair and builds on each partner's experience.
Consortium Management **structure** will consist of:
Project overall coordinator - The coordinator will initiate regular e-mail group contact, including the establishment of an online communication platform to which all partners will be required to contribute. This will ensure ongoing communications and awareness of the progress being made by all partners, as well as a sharing of good ideas.
Workpackage management group – The leader of each workpackage and the coordinator will form the WP management group, whose will be to ensure that each workpackage is carried out in full, that all partners participate and that targets and deliverables are realized. Each management group will have to participate in meeting that will take

place at least once during the lifetime of the WP, in order to discuss the related to the WP issues.\
Project full consortium – Consisting of all members of the consortium, responsible for delivery of their own defined work programmes providing activity and financial reports to deadlines, participating in consortium meetings.

WP1200: Assessment of Progress and Results
WP Responsible: IDEC
The project management has a central role for the success of the project, in that support and guides the consortium in developing a correct and effective running of the activities. In addition, the management framework enabled in the market validation phase will constitute the basis for the management of the overall project, thus also in the deployment phase, with the aim of structuring the needed relationships and procedures.

WP2000: Toolbox Platform Design
WP Responsible: UNIROMA1
The objective of this WP is to provide the EUGAGER development phase with the identification of potential users and their requirements, and the definition of services and utilization scenario, including the guidelines for data management and future exploitation. Moreover, a prototype implementation of the core platform and the authentication tool will be delivered.
The WP is divided into the following second-level-WPs.

WP2100: Requirements Analysis
WP Responsible: UNIROMA1
This second-level WP deals with Requirements analysis as for knowledge, security and transparency on top of which our platform will stand. The process of analysis will drive us to the definition of the requirements needed by the platform and to the definition of the system architecture.
The objective of this WP is to identify the requirements of the system, concerning the three main areas addressed by the project: Knowledge, Security and Transparency.
In particular, Security requirements analysis will be addressed by a specific subtask of the WP, and it will comprise also a comprehensive

threat analysis to identify the possible threats and vulnerability of the architecture.

User, service, platform and application requirements will be identified following phase of Toolbox and Tool Design. The platform requirements will be addressed by a specific subtask of this WP, considering especially the security, privacy and trustworthiness requirements that the platform should guarantee.

The overall architecture of the system will be defined in a specific subtask of this WP.

WP2200: Toolbox Design
WP Responsible: UNIROMA1

We will design the APIs to be used by the collaborative proposal tool and by all the other applications that will be developed within the project. The API will allow tools to perform only well-defined and restrictive operations on the data and structures inside the toolbox, to assure the trustworthiness of the platform and to avoid that a malicious application can perform dangerous operations. We will design the database architecture and data formats, and then a prototype will be implemented following these requirements.

WP2300: Toolbox Tools Design
WP Responsible: TFF

The objective is to build a first prototype of the applications that will rely on the EUGAGER platform. To this aim, we will first build the authentication and tool manager. Then, we will define the EUGAGER Tools Markup Language, in order to specify the markup language accepted by EUGAGER Tools. Finally, we will implement the User Profile, Preferences and Activity Feed, where users will have a broader view on their activity within EUGAGER, the tools they use, the people they connect and the constituency domains they belong to. Users will have access to their activity stream also in RSS format.

WP3000: Knowledge
WP Responsible: FCTUC

In this WP we will coordinate efforts for the design and implementation of the knowledge-related applications. To this aim, a number of workshops/meetings will be organized for the coordination between FCTUC and UBO.

WP3100: Collaborative Filtering and Knowledge Sharing
WP Responsible: UBO

In this WP a multidimensional recommender system will be researched and formally described. Therefore a multidimensional rating system has to be developed to create user profiles. Similarity measures are important for collaborative filtering techniques and must be evolved in respect to multiple dimensions. Domain dependencies will also be explored using collaborative approaches to find new rating weights for different (unknown) domains of items automatically.

WP3200: Knowledge Learning and Tracking with Folksonomy
WP Responsible: FCTUC

In WP2260 we implemented a broad folksonomy, giving to users the possibility to tag different resources. Here we shall use the information generated to produce a graph of the information inserted (proposals, petitions, others -eventually-). Based on this graph we will permit to users to find related information, respect to a resource. Search information based on an ordered set of keywords, and order all the information in mutually exclusive clusters that shall both represent the information entered, and the culture of the people that entered that information.

WP3300: Knowledge Creation
WP Responsible: FCTUC

Given a system that permit to different users to propose different answers to a given question, we shall investigate, and implement an algorithm that permit to users to endorse each other solution, and provide new solutions, based on the existing ones. The system as a whole should work as a human based genetic algorithm, where users shall insert different solutions, and the users shall also evaluate each other solution. Two different possibilities will be investigated, although more could appear as part of the research.

WP4000: Security
WP Responsible: UNIROMA1

This WP will address all the issues concerning the security and privacy research efforts necessary to achieve a proper degree of trustworthiness of the entire system.
The WP is divided into the following second-level-WPs.

WP4100: Protocols and Policies Design
WP Responsible: UNIROMA1

The objective of this WP is to design all the Security Protocols and Policies to guarantee the overall system security. In particular, the following research issues will be addressed:

- design of on a suitable new protocol for user's authentication. This protocol should guarantee a high level of security, even preserving a high degree of usability, scalability, efficiency, and low costs.
- use of a RBAC (Role Based Access Control) methodology to guarantee from misuse of the platform. The Policies will be defined according to the reference context. Also, constituency domains will be implemented using roles. The role configuration system will be devised to the precise definition of the set of users allowed to create constituency domains and to install and run applications on the platform
- Integrity and Confidentiality Enforcement, through the design of suitable protocols

WP4200: Protocols and Policies Formal Verification
WP Responsible: UNIROMA1

In this work package we plan to formally verify, by using model checking techniques, all the protocols designed in WP4100. This will provide us with a mathematical proof of correctness for the e-government toolbox and applications we are building. Moreover, also we plan to build a framework allowing us to automatically synthesize a desired access control policy with respect to high-level specifications.

WP4300: Privacy Management
WP Responsible: UNIROMA1

In this work package we plan to define, design and implement all the issues regarding the user privacy management when using applications based on our EUGAGER platform. When dealing with privacy, we should take care of two aspects. On one side, we should guarantee the privacy of the user. On the other side, we should control the access to private data. In order to achieve these goals, the privacy management thus entails a requirements analysis, architecture definition and final implementation for both the toolbox user privacy management and the private data access control policies.

WP5000: Transparency
WP Responsible: UBO
This WP concerns the research activities in developments of new approach to increase transparency. Each research activity is represented by a sub-WP. The sub-WPs include also the design and development of the software tools to be added to the toolbox

WP5100: Raw Data Verifiability
WP Responsible: UNIROMA1
The aim of this WP is to design a methodology that allows users to track the correctness of the raw data and integrate it in the toolbox implementation.
We plan to achieve this goal establishing a protocol of interaction between (generally untrusted) tools and the (trusted) toolbox: tools may acquire sensible data (e.g. endorsement) in encrypted form and decrypt it only by using suitable toolbox APIs. Toolbox must store sensible data in trusted databases.
In the same way, sensible activity (e.g. identification) must be accomplished invoking toolbox APIs.

WP5200: Tool Results Verifiability
WP Responsible: UNIROMA1
Stemming from the raw data correctness (WP5100) users and government should be able to verify tools results. To this end, in this WP we plan to define a formalism to allow tools to formally specify relationships between raw data and their outputs. Moreover, we will implement a verifier that automatically checks if tool results meet specification. Security issues, such as privacy and secrecy, will be carefully considered.

WP5300: Evaluation of Information Filtering Technologies
WP Responsible: UBO
This WP contains the creation of test collection from the user profiles. Therefore the gathered user data has to be processed into a uniform test collection and the given rating dimensions have to be described. To evaluate the functionality of the recommender system, appropriate evaluation measures have to be chosen, adjusted and described. Then the evaluation functionality has to be implemented resulting in an evaluation framework for this test collection. The evaluation results will be presented and interpreted in an appropriate way.

WP6000: Prototype & Demonstrations
WP Responsible: TFF
This WP will address the demonstration (testing) and prototyping activities to populate the EUGAGER platform with basic tools for user interaction.

The WP is divided into the following second-level-WPs.

WP6100: Collaborative Proposal Tool
WP Responsible: TESIA
Objectives
In this developmental WP the ideas of knowledge creation researched in WP3300 will be implemented. This will happen in two separate instances. First in a standalone test case, that will permit to provide a tool for the first explorative research to be done. The program will be released in open source, and actively maintained, while the core EUGAGE is being implemented. In order to achieve this goal, a requirements analysis will be performed, followed by a design and implementation phase.
As a second step, a second version will be presented as a final application that ties into the core EUGAGER. This version will be tested to be able to support enough users to be usable at a national level.

WP6200: Petition Tool
WP Responsible: TFF
An Online e-Petition tool that enable users to create and sign petitions. Petitions can define the constituency domain they belong to (i.e.: Italian citizens; French Citizens; Residents in the City of Rome, etc...). The Petitions API will enable users of other tools (i.e.: the Collaborative Proposal Tool) to read, create or sign petitions without leaving their workspace.

WP6300: Toolbox Integration and Testing
WP Responsible: TESIA
The Platform and its integration with the tools developed will be tested and evaluated by a group of users before the final release.

WP6400: Collaborative Information Filtering

WP Responsible: UBO
This WP contains the implementation of the Collaborative Information
Filtering approach which is researched and described within WP3100.

WP7000: Dissemination and Exploitation
WP Responsible: IDEC
The objective of this WP is to coordinate the dissemination and the
exploitation of EUGAGER. More details are given in the following
WPs.

WP7100: Dissemination
WP Responsible: IDEC
Objective of this workpackage is to disseminate the EUGAGER project
in national and international level in order to further enhance the use of
its results. The main aims of the dissemination are:
> 1) the engagement of the target groups and lobbying of key
> actors in the realisation process of the project.
> 2) to inform the public of the project results.
> 3) to raise awareness towards the project related issues

Target groups of the dissemination activities will be both the scientific
community and beneficiaries among the general public.
Throughout the scientific community, the objective will be to promote
EUGAGER tools and services to lead to better networking between
scientists in and out of the knowledge, transparency and security
research fields, from European Member States.
As for the general public (including both citizens and governments), the
dissemination will aim at enhancing their awareness on the great
chances offered by the existence of a platform allowing the
empowerment and engagement of all types of societal groups and
communities in policy-making processes.

WP7200: Exploitation
WP Responsible: FCTUC
Aim of this workpackage is to set the base for the use and
mainstreaming of the project results.
Due to the extensive network of associates that all project partners have
throughout Europe, the exploitation strategy will also focus on the

possibilities for mainstreaming the project's products in countries other than the ones participating in the project.

The exploitation will be based in a set of tools that will include demonstration of project products at events, promotion of web site, distribution of brochures, mailing, faxes etc. The exploitation and dissemination strategies and objectives are quite similar, therefore some activities will interlay and will provide valuable feedback for both workpackages.

Expected outcomes of the workpackage are an exploitation plan and a number of exploitation activities. The exploitation plan will include the general exploitation strategy of the project,. Responsible for its development is IDEC (P1). All partners will have to participate in exploitation activities and report them to IDEC. The overall exploitation activities will be published on the website at the end of the project.

Table 1.3-d - Work Packages Description

Work package number	WP1000	Start date or starting event:		Month 1		
Work package title	Project Management and Coordination					
Activity type	MGT					
Participant number	1	2	3	4	5	6
Participant short name	IDEC	UNIROMA1	TFF	FCTUC	TESIA	UBO
Person-months per participant	1	0	0	0	0	0

Objectives

Management and Coordination of the whole EUGAGER project, especially for the EU interface

Description of work

T1010 - Ensure technical and contractual interface with EU

T1020 - Provide guidelines to partners, for the execution of their activities in accordance with EU guidelines, and control performance and progress.

T1030 - Preparation of inputs for project reviews according to the EU Call

T1040 - Report project progress and status to EU.

T1050 - Identify events which could affect the achievement of the project objectives, and plan recovery actions.

T1060 - Scheduling, reporting and train - Its support staff to meet all EU requirements

Deliverables		
Del. no.	**Deliverable name**	**Delivery (proj. month)**
D1001	Periodic Activity Report	6, 12, 18, 24, 30, 36
D1002	Updated Implementation Plan	The first implementation plan is the proposal itself. Then according to the results of the periodic activity reports and the needs of the consortium there will be adjustments and updates to the implementation plan. A proposed delivery date is one per year.

Work package number	WP1100	Start date or starting event:		Month 1		
Work package title	Consortium Management					
Activity type	MGT					
Participant number	1	2	3	4	5	6
Participant short name	IDEC	UNIROMA1	TFF	FCTUC	TESIA	UBO
Person-months per participant	4	0	0	0	0	0

Objectives

Management and Coordination of the consortium for EUGAGER project

- Management of the project in agreement with EU direction.

- Control of progress and performance

- Establish the contractual framework for the relationship between the parties involved

Description of work

Overall coordination:

T1110 - Ensure that resources (manpower/material, etc.) are available
for the successful performance of the project.

T1120 - Evaluation of project performance, identification of
deficiencies/inadequacies, and implementation of corrective
actions; control project progress.

T1130 - Identify events which could affect the achievement of the
project objectives, and plan recovery actions.

T1140 - Interface and manage information flow among all the project
Tasks

T1150 - Ensure the timeliness of all the deliverables.

Contract and Financial Management:

T1160 - Monitor the Annual Cost Statements

T1170 - Attendance in team meetings monitoring the compliance with
contractual conditions

T1180 - Advise project manager on contractual status and implications

T1190 - Initialise invoicing and payment on request or approval of the
project manager

Deliverables		
Del. no.	**Deliverable name**	**Delivery (proj. month)**
D1101	Financial Plan	1
D1102	Management Report	6, 12, 18, 24, 30, 36
D1103	Communication Platform	1

Work package number	WP1200	Start date or starting event:			Month 7	
Work package title	Assessment of Progress and Results					
Activity type	MGT					
Participant number	1	2	3	4	5	6
Participant short name	IDEC	UNIROMA1	TFF	FCTUC	TESIA	UBO
Person-months per participant	4	0	0	2	0	0

Objectives

Assessment of Progress and Results for EUGAGER project

- Delivery of the requested documentation
- Control & Reporting
- Documentation Management

Description of work
Overall coordination:
T1210 - Preparation of inputs for project reviews according to the EU Call
T1220 - Perform and document project meetings with project team
T1230 - Documentation Management
T1240 - Establishment of documentation and document control guidelines and procedures

Deliverables

Del. no.	Deliverable name	Delivery (proj. month)
D1201	Documentation Management Report	1

Work package number	WP2000	Start date or starting event:		Month 1	
Work package title	Toolbox Platform Design				
Activity type	MGT				
Participant number	1	2	3	4	5	6
Participant short name	IDEC	UNIROMA1	TFF	FCTUC	TESIA	UBO
Person-months per participant	0	1	0	0	0	0

Objectives

The objective is to coordinate efforts for the whole EUGAGER development phase.

Description of work

T2010 - Co-ordination: WP2200 and WP2300 are relatively independently of each other, but depend upon WP2100. A number of workshops/meetings will be organized for the coordination.

Deliverables

Del. no.	Deliverable name	Delivery (proj. month)
D2011	Coordination document	1, 12

Work package number	WP2100	Start date or starting event:			Month 1	
Work package title	Requirements Analysis					
Activity type	RTD					
Participant number	1	2	3	4	5	6
Participant short name	IDEC	UNIROMA1	TFF	FCTUC	TESIA	UBO
Person-months per participant	0	1,5	1,75	2,5	0,75	2,5

Objectives

The objective is to collect all the requirements we need for the several aspects of EUGAGER, namely knowledge, security, transparency, and their relationships with the architecture of the EUGAGER platform.

Description of work

T2110 - Knowledge Requirement Analysis. The objective is to collect the knowledge requirements, especially in the EUnomia toolbox application.

T2120 - Security Requirement Analysis: The objective is to collect the security requirements.

T2130 - Transparency Requirement Analysis: The objective is to collect the transparency requirements, especially in the communications between end users and the toolbox.

T2140 - Platform Requirement Analysis: The objective is to collect the requirements necessary to satisfy EUGAGER Platform features.

Deliverables		
Del. no.	**Deliverable name**	**Delivery (proj. month)**
D2141	Requirements Description	3

Work package number	WP2200	Start date or starting event:				Month 4
Work package title	Toolbox Design					
Activity type	RTD					
Participant number	1	2	3	4	5	6
Participant short name	IDEC	UNIROMA1	TFF	FCTUC	TESIA	UBO
Person-months per participant	0	1,5	6	9	8	8,5

Objectives

The objective is to build a first prototype of the EUGAGER platform, by defining its components. We plan to implement a first version of the EUGAGER APIs (D2231) and then to refine it (D2232).

Description of work

T2210 - Architecture Definition: the objective is to define and document the architecture for the EUGAGER Platform Core and its relation with EUGAGER Tools.

T2220 -EUGAGER API Definition: we will define an Application Program Interface for EUGAGER, so that the tools can call standard API methods to interface with the core primitives and/or the user profile (i.e.: calling users.getInfo to retrieve a user's authorized information and display it)

T2230 - Database Modelling: the objective is to design the internal database for the EUGAGER platform

T2240 - Implementation of EUGAGER API: the objective is to design the interface between the EUGAGER platform and the toolbox applications

T2250 - Implementation of Core Prototype: we will implement the web interface of EUGAGER that users will call from their tools. The core contains and uses the EUGAGER API previously developed.

T2260 - Implementation of Broad folksonomy in the core: a module will be developed that permit to users to bookmark and tag objects (proposals, petitions, others) in EUGAGER. The information generated by this module will eventually (WP3100) permit to track the generated knowledge, and facilitate the search of the relevant information.

T2270 - Implementation of multidimensional rating functionality: this task involves the implementation of the rating functionality for the user and the management of user profiles.

Deliverables

Del. no.	Deliverable name	Delivery (proj. month)
D2211	Toolbox Platform Architecture Documentation	4
D2221	EUGAGER API Definition	10
D2231	EUGAGER Core Database Model	9
D2232	EUGAGER API v1	11
D2241	EUGAGER API v2	14

Deliverables		
Del. no.	**Deliverable name**	**Delivery (proj. month)**
D2261	EUGAGER Core Platform Prototype	17

Work package number	WP2300	Start date or starting event:				Month 9
Work package title	Toolbox Tools Design					
Activity type	RTD					
Participant number	1	2	3	4	5	6
Participant short name	IDEC	UNIROMA1	TFF	FCTUC	TESIA	UBO
Person-months per participant	0	1	10,25	2,5	1,75	2,5

Objectives

The objective is to build a first prototype of the applications that will rely on the EUGAGER platform.

Description of work

T2310 - Requirements Analysis for Authentication and Tool Manager: we will investigate and document the requirements necessary to build the system for user Authentication ("secure" for verifying users real identity and "non-secure" for regular login) and the Tool Manager, where users and governments can register/unregister new tools (and receive an API key to use within their tool) and manage the Tools they are subscribed to (search/add/remove).

T2320 - Architecture Definition for Authentication and Tool Manager: we will define and document the architecture to implement the Authentication and Tool Manager and its relation with the EUGAGER Core.

T2330 - EUGAGER Tools Markup Language Definition: we will define limitations and/or modifications in the markup language accepted by EUGAGER Tools, to permit automated control and detection of malicious code.

T2340 - Implementation of Authentication and Tool Manager: we will implement the Authentication and Tool Manager screens, using the EUGAGER API.

T2350 - Implementation of User Profile, Preferences and Activity Feed: we will implement the User Profile Page and Activity Feed, where users will have a broader view on their activity within EUGAGER, the tools they use, the people they connect and the constituency domains they belong to. Users will have access to their activity stream also in RSS format. We will also implement the User Preferences screen where users will be able to set default privacy and notification preferences that apply to all newly added tools.

Deliverables

Del. no.	Deliverable name	Delivery (proj. month)
D2311	Authentication and Tool Manager Architecture Documentation	16
D2341	Authentication and Tool Manager Prototype	20

Deliverables		
Del. no.	**Deliverable name**	**Delivery (proj. month)**
D2351	User Profile and Preferences Page	18
D2352	User Activity Stream Page	20

Work package number	WP3000	Start date or starting event:				Month 7
Work package title	Knowledge					
Activity type	RTD					
Participant number	1	2	3	4	5	6
Participant short name	IDEC	UNIROMA1	TFF	FCTUC	TESIA	UBO
Person-months per participant	0	0	0	1	0	0

Objectives

The objective is to coordinate efforts for the design and implementation of the knowledge-related applications.

Description of work

T3010 - Co-ordination: A number of workshops/meetings will be organized for the coordination between FCTUC and UBO.

Deliverables		
Del. no.	Deliverable name	Delivery (proj. month)
D3011	Coordination document	7, 19

Work package number	WP3100	Start date or starting event:			Month 7	
Work package title	Collaborative Filtering and Knowledge Sharing					
Activity type	RTD					
Participant number	1	2	3	4	5	6
Participant short name	IDEC	UNIROMA1	TFF	FCTUC	TESIA	UBO
Person-months per participant	0	0	0	3	0	30

Objectives

The objective is to research and describe a multidimensional recommender system which aim is to propose new available items concerning the user. Collaborative approaches to adjust the weightings of the multiple rating dimensions will be explored for this purpose.

Description of work

T3110- R&D of a multidimensional rating system for user content: the multiple dimensions of ratings have to be described and explored and a reasonable subset has to be chosen for the user profile creation. The problems of scalability, data integrity, privacy and security concerns must be solved.

T3120 - Analysis of rating-dimensions and object-dependencies: the set of rating dimensions will be researched in respect of their characteristics and interdependencies. The mapping of object-classes to different dimension weightings must be examined and may lead to weighting templates. Another aim is to find ways to create such templates for new unknown classes in an automated way and by user collaboration.

T3130 - R&D on uses of similarity between users by tag uses: we will research similarity measures based on the tags created by the users.

T3140 - R&D of similarity measures: this task involves the research of multiple similarity measures based on the multidimensional ratings stored in user profiles.

T3150 - R&D of trust measures: Because the user of EUGAGER is able to stay anonym in unsecure applications we have to consider users with bad intentions (e.g. spammers) which cannot be trusted. We will therefore explore the possibility of trust measurement based on the user profiles and possible given graphs of neighbourhood (of similar users).

T3160 - Statistical analysis of user behaviour & Clustering: The statistical analysis of actual users´ behaviour in the running system should provide motivation and ideas for new approaches of collaboration in information retrieval and in the European society.

Deliverables		
Del. no.	**Deliverable name**	**Delivery (proj. month)**
D3111	Results of the R&D of a multidimensional rating system for user content	3
D3121	Analysis of rating-dimensions	18

Deliverables		
Del. no.	**Deliverable name**	**Delivery (proj. month)**
	and object-dependencies (results)	
D3131	Description of similarity measures based on users´ tags	33
D3141	Description of similarity measures on multidimensional ratings	33
D3151	Trust Algorithm Description	33
D3161	Statistical Analysis Results	35

Work package number	WP3200	Start date or starting event:			Month 19
Work package title	Knowledge Learning and Tracking with Folksonomy				
Activity type	RTD				
Participant number	1	2	3	4	5	6
Participant short name	IDEC	UNIROMA1	TFF	FCTUC	TESIA	UBO
Person-months per participant	0	0	0	20	2,5	0

Objectives

In WP2260 we implemented a broad folksonomy, giving to users the possibility to tag different resources. Here we shall use the information generated to produce a graph of the information inserted (proposals, petitions, others -eventually-). Based on this graph we will permit to users to find related information, respect to a resource. Search information based on an ordered set of keywords, and order all the information in mutually exclusive clusters that shall both represent the information entered, and the culture of the people that entered that information.

Description of work

T3210 - R&D on the graph of near objects: R&D on the graph of near objects: The graph of the objects inserted in EUGAGER shall be produced. Such graph should be produced using the metric generated by the implementer broad folksonomy. Two objects would be linked if one is the n-th nearest neighbours of the other. When a user is observing an object, a pointer toward the information about the linked object should also be made available.

T3220 - R&D of a tag based search engine: The possibility to insert an ordered list of tags, and receive the most relevant objects, should be inserted. This should be based on the tags the users have inserted

T3230 - R&D on Clustering of Application Objects: An analysis of the graph on a global level should be done, of its clusters, and the list of clusters will be presented as a top down way to investigate the existing objects

T3240 - R&D on Endorsing by Proxy near a point in Folksonomy space: The possibility to users to permit to other users to be their representatives in some contexts shall be inserted. This should be done by letting users select an area of expertise (as an ordered set of tags), and select a user, who will then decide what to endorse in that context.

T3250 - Research on the Relation Clusters vs. Culture: As clusters represent the culture of the users that tagged the objects, we shall confront the clusters generated by users from different cultures, trying to establish what information, if any, are those clusters providing us about the original culture.

Deliverables

Del. no.	Deliverable name	Delivery (proj. month)
D3211	Graph Generation Algorithm Description and Analysis of Performance	21
D3221	Search Algorithm Description and Analysis of Performance	24
D3231	Emergent Clusters Analysis and Analysis of Performance	27
D3241	Similarity Measures Description	35
D3251	Communities Clusters Comparison Report	32
D3252	Extracted Information Analysis	35

Work package number	WP3300	Start date or starting event:			Month 7	
Work package title	Knowledge Creation					
Activity type	RTD					
Participant number	1	2	3	4	5	6
Participant short name	IDEC	UNIROMA1	TFF	FCTUC	TESIA	UBO
Person-months per participant	0	0	0	29	2	0

Objectives

Given a system that permit to different users to propose different answers to a given question, we shall investigate, and implement an algorithm that permit to users to endorse each other solution, and provide new solutions, based on the existing ones. The system as a whole should work as a human based genetic algorithm, where users shall insert different solutions, and the users shall also evaluate each other solution. Two different possibilities will be investigated, although more could appear as part of the research.

Description of work

T3310 - R&D the Pareto Front Endorsing System: Requirement Analysis: an analysis of the requirement (technical and social) under which it is possible to apply and utilise the Pareto Front Endorsing System.

T3320 - R&D the Pareto Front Endorsing System: Methodology Design. We shall produce an algorithm, where users go through subsequent rounds of production of new proposals, and evaluation of each other proposals. The resulting, evaluated, proposals will be analysed, and when one proposals (in terms of who voted it) clearly dominates another, the dominated one will be discarded. The resulting set will represent a Pareto Front of proposals, and shall be used as the seed for the next generations

T3330 - R&D the Pareto Front Endorsing System: Result Analysis. The system shall be implemented (in WP6100), and the results shall then, here be analysed.

T3340 - R&D the Continuous Darwinian Genetic Algorithm: Requirement Analysis. An analysis of the requirement (technical and social) under which it is possible to apply and utilise the Continuous Darwinian Genetic Algorithm.

T3350 - R&D the Continuous Darwinian Genetic Algorithm: Methodology Design. We shall produce an algorithm where users shall be allowed to insert new proposals on an ongoing basis. Links between related proposals shall be inserted, and ways to let new proposals not be disadvantaged respect to the older ones shall be researched. Possible ways might advertising the new proposals in a way that is proportional to the level of endorsement that a proposal get respect to the existing, older proposals. Other possibilities might be considered.

T3360 - R&D the Continuous Darwinian Genetic Algorithm: Results Analysis. The system shall be implemented (in WP6100), and the results shall then, here be analysed

Deliverables		
Del. no.	**Deliverable name**	**Delivery (proj. month)**
D3311	Pareto Front Genetic Algorithm Description	12
D3312	Pareto Front Results Description	2 4
D3321	Continuous Genetic Algorithms Description	18
D3222	Continuous Genetic Algorithms Results	30

Work package number	WP4000	Start date or starting event:				Month 9
Work package title	Security					
Activity type	RTD					
Participant number	1	2	3	4	5	6
Participant short name	IDEC	UNIROMA1	TFF	FCTUC	TESIA	UBO
Person-months per participant	0	1	0	0	0	0

Objectives

The objective is to design safe, reliable and trustworthy protocols for the toolbox, that will be designed to assure an adequate level of security and to guarantee the properties of confidentiality and integrity of information, identity and access control, privacy of users. It will be formally proven (verified) that the proposed system does have the above properties, notwithstanding malicious attacks (misuse). Finally, all the privacy issues will be taken into consideration and solved.

Description of work

T4010 - Coordinate Protocols Definition and Verification: the objective is to coordinate efforts between definition of protocols and their verification, e.g. to ensure that the correct assumptions are made when modelling protocols.

Deliverables

Del. no.	Deliverable name	Delivery (proj. month)
D4011	Coordination document	9, 18

Work package number	WP4100	Start date or starting event:				Month 9
Work package title	Protocols and Policies Design					
Activity type	RTD					
Participant number	1	2	3	4	5	6
Participant short name	IDEC	UNIROMA1	TFF	FCTUC	TESIA	UBO
Person-months per participant	0	16	0	0	0	0

Objectives

The objective is to design safe, reliable and trustworthy protocols for the toolbox, that will be designed to assure an adequate level of security and to guarantee the properties of confidentiality and integrity of information, identity and access control, privacy of users.

Description of work

T4110 - Authentication Protocol Design: we will start from deliverable D2141 to design a new Authentication Protocol that assures both weak and strong authentication. We will focus also on usability of the whole mechanism.

T4120 - Access Control Policies Design: we will limit the access to the services provided by the toolbox by defining a Role Based Access Control. Policies should be restrictive enough to prevent a misuse of the resources, while allowing toolbox and tools to have significant interactions

T4130 - Integrity Evaluation and Design: starting from the analysis of the security requirements performed in T2120, we will define the protocols and mechanisms that will be implemented to assure a satisfactory degree of integrity of data and services used within the entire architecture. This will be done through the use of mechanisms such as digital signatures, hashed functions, message authentication codes (MAC), message integrity codes (MIC), leading to the design of novel methods based on well-known integrity mechanisms.

T4140 - Confidentiality Evaluation and Design: starting from the analysis of the security requirements performed in T2120, we will define the protocols and mechanisms that will be implemented to assure a satisfactory degree of confidentiality of data stored and exchanged within the entire architecture. This will be done through the use of mechanisms such as symmetric or asymmetric cryptography, leading to the design of novel methods based on well-known confidentiality mechanisms.

Deliverables		
Del. no.	**Deliverable name**	**Delivery (proj. month)**
D4111	Authentication Protocol Description	16
D4121	Access Control Policies Description	16
D4141	Integrity and Confidentiality Report	21

Work package number	WP4200	Start date or starting event:			Month 16	
Work package title	Protocols and Policies Formal Verification					
Activity type	RTD					
Participant number	1	2	3	4	5	6
Participant short name	IDEC	UNIROMA1	TFF	FCTUC	TESIA	UBO
Person-months per participant	0	11	0,75	0	0	0

Objectives

The objective is to formally verify that the proposed system (EUGAGER platform + toolbox applications) does ensure security, notwithstanding malicious attacks (misuse). This will be done by verifying via model checking the security protocols and control access rules given in WP4100. We will also design a methodology to automatically synthesize control access rules.

Description of work

T4210 - Authentication Protocol Verification: the protocols designed in T4110 will be formally verified by using Model Checking techniques.

T4220 - Access Control Policies Verification: the Access Control Policies defined in T4120 will be formally verified by using Model Checking techniques. This will allow us to formally verify both that applications would not misuse our APIs, and that applications would indeed be able to achieve legitimate goals.

T4230 - Access Control Policies Automatic Synthesis: we plan to design a tool for automatic synthesis of control access rules from a given specification. The specification may describe a legitimate goal (and in this case we are interested in the most restrictive set of rules) or a property that all user interactions must satisfy (and in this case we are interested in the most liberal set of rules). To this end we plan to use ideas from controller synthesis algorithm and supervisory control synthesis.

T4240 - Web Application Security Analysis: we will use standard tools and guidelines to measure the security of our applications.

Deliverables		
Del. no.	**Deliverable name**	**Delivery (proj. month)**
D4211	Authentication Protocol Verification Description	18
D4221	Access Control Policies Verification Description	18
D4222	Access Control Policies Verification Tool	21
D4231	Access Control Policies Automatic Synthesis Description	19
D4232	Access Control Policies Automatic Synthesis Tool	21

Deliverables		
Del. no.	**Deliverable name**	**Delivery (proj. month)**
D4241	Web Application Security Analysis Results	17

Work package number	WP4300	Start date or starting event:			Month 13	
Work package title	Privacy Management					
Activity type	RTD					
Participant number	1	2	3	4	5	6
Participant short name	IDEC	UNIROMA1	TFF	FCTUC	TESIA	UBO
Person-months per participant	0	9	3,25	0,5	0	0

Objectives

The objective is to define, design and implement all the issues regarding the user privacy management when using applications based on our EUGAGER platform.

Description of work

T4310 - Requirements Analysis for Toolbox User Privacy Management: we will investigate and document the requirements to satisfy the users privacy concerns when using EUGAGER such as granting access to specific tools, managing invites to connect with others, profile visibility and personal content licensing.

T4320 - Architecture Definition for Toolbox User Privacy Management: we will define and document the architecture for the Toolbox User Privacy Management system and its relation to EUGAGER core and EUGAGER tools.

T4330 - Implementation of Granular User Privacy Controls: we will implement granular user privacy controls, such as providing the user with the ability to choose which data from her profile can be accessed by each application or visible in searches, blocking individual applications and users, suspending or deleting her account.

T4340 - Requirements Analysis for Tools Private Data Access Controls: we will identify and document the requirements needed to implement the Private Data Access Control system used by EUGAGER to selectively provide information to tools requesting it via API (e.g. controlling user blocks on specific tools, monitoring granular privacy rules set by the user via the User Preferences screen, etc).

T4350 - Architecture Definition for Tools Private Data Access Controls: we will define and document the architecture for the Private Data Access Control system used by EUGAGER Tools to request information from EUGAGER Core via the API previously released.

T4360 - Implementation of Tools Private Data Access Controls: we will implementing the web interface for the Tools Private Data Access Controls.

Deliverables		
Del. no.	**Deliverable name**	**Delivery (proj. month)**
D4311	Requirements Analysis for Toolbox User Privacy Management Description	16
D4321	Architecture Definition for Toolbox User Privacy Management Documentation	19
D4331	Tools Supporting Granular User Privacy Controls	24
D4341	Requirements Analysis for Tools Private Data Access Controls Definition	16
D4351	Architecture for Tools Private Data Access Controls Documentation	19
D4361	Implementation of Tools Private Data Access Controls	24

Work package number	WP5000	Start date or starting event:			Month 18
Work package title	Transparency				
Activity type	RTD				
Participant number	1	2	3	4	5	6
Participant short name	IDEC	UNIROMA1	TFF	FCTUC	TESIA	UBO
Person-months per participant	0	0	0	0	0	1

Objectives

The objective is to coordinate efforts to define a new approach to increase transparency in e-government applications.

Description of work

T5010 – Coordination: A number of workshops/meetings will be organized for the coordination between UNIROMA1 and UBO.

Deliverables

Del. no.	Deliverable name	Delivery (proj. month)
D5011	Coordination document	21, 28

Work package number	WP5100	Start date or starting event:				Month 18
Work package title	Raw Data Verifiability					
Activity type	RTD					
Participant number	1	2	3	4	5	6
Participant short name	IDEC	UNIROMA1	TFF	FCTUC	TESIA	UBO
Person-months per participant	0	7	0,5	2	0	0

Objectives

The objective is to design a methodology that allow users to track the correctness of their raw data and integrate it in the toolbox implementation.

Description of work

T5110 - Requirement Analysis: the objective is to collect the requirements needed to let the user track its raw data.

T5120 - Methodology Design: we plan to achieve this goal establishing a protocol of interaction between (generally untrusted) tools and the (trusted) toolbox: tools may acquire sensible data (e.g. endorsement) in encrypted form and decrypt it only by using suitable toolbox APIs. Toolbox must store sensible data in trusted databases. In the same way, sensible activity (e.g. identification) must be accomplished invoking toolbox APIs.

T5130 - Implementation: we will implement the methodology outlined in task T5120.

Deliverables		
Del. no.	**Deliverable name**	**Delivery (proj. month)**
D5111	Requirements Analysis Description	19
D5121	Methodology Design Description	28
D5131	Tool for Raw Data Verifiability	35

Work package number	WP5200	Start date or starting event:			Month 21	
Work package title	Tool Results Verifiability					
Activity type	RTD					
Participant number	1	2	3	4	5	6
Participant short name	IDEC	UNIROMA1	TFF	FCTUC	TESIA	UBO
Person-months per participant	0	7	0,5	2	0	0

Objectives

The objective is to define a formalism to allow tools to formally specify relationships between raw data and their outputs, and to design and implement a verifier that automatically checks if tool results meet specifications.

Description of work

T5210 - Requirement Analysis: we will identify and document the requirements needed to design and implement a verifier to automatically check if tool results meet specifications.

T5220 - Methodology Design: we will define and document the architecture and design for a methodology to verify if tool results meet specifications.

T5230 - Implementation: we will implement the methodology outlined in task T5220.

Deliverables		
Del. no.	Deliverable name	Delivery (proj. month)

D5211	Requirements Analysis Description	22
D5221	Methodology Design Description	30
D5231	Tool for Application Results Verifiability	35

Work package number	WP5300	Start date or starting event:			Month 29	
Work package title	Evaluation of Information Filtering Technologies					
Activity type	RTD					
Participant number	1	2	3	4	5	6
Participant short name	IDEC	UNIROMA1	TFF	FCTUC	TESIA	UBO
Person-months per participant	0	0	0	0	0	6

Objectives

The objective comprises the creation of a test collection from the user profiles and the thorough evaluation of the researched information filtering concepts.

Description of work

T5310 - Creation of test collection from processed user profiles: the gathered user data has to be processed into a uniform test collection.

T5320 - Definition of Evaluation Measures: to evaluate the functionality of the recommender system, appropriate evaluation measures have to be chosen, adjusted and described.

T5330 - Implementation and Presentation of results: this includes the implementation of the evaluation functionality and the presentation and interpretation of the results.

Deliverables

Del. no.	Deliverable name	Delivery (proj. month)

D5311	Test collection from processed user profiles	34
D5321	Description of Evaluation procedure	32
D5331	Implementation and results	36

Work package number	WP6000	Start date or starting event:				Month 6	
Work package title	Prototype & Demonstrations						
Activity type	DEM						
Participant number	1	2	3	4	5	6	
Participant short name	IDEC	UNIROMA1	TFF	FCTUC	TESIA	UBO	
Person-months per participant	0	0	1	0	0	0	

Objectives

The objective is to build prototypes for all the software designed in the project, in order to test them and to give demonstrations.

Description of work

T6010 – Coordinate: it is necessary to coordinate the efforts for the implementations of the different parts of the EUGAGER platform and toolbox applications.

Deliverables

Del. no.	Deliverable name	Delivery (proj. month)
D6011	Coordination document	6, 18, 26

Work package number	WP6100	Start date or starting event:			Month 6	
Work package title	Collaborative Proposal Tool					
Activity type	DEM					
Participant number	1	2	3	4	5	6
Participant short name	IDEC	UNIROMA1	TFF	FCTUC	TESIA	UBO
Person-months per participant	0	0	0	9	21,5	0

Objectives

In this developmental work package the ideas of knowledge creation researched in WP3300 will be implemented. This will happen in two separate instances. First in a standalone test case, that will permit to provide a tool for the first explorative research to be done. The program will be released in open source, and actively maintained, while the core EUGAGE is being implemented; then as a final application that ties into the core EUGAGER, a second version will be presented. This version will be tested to be able to support enough users to be usable at a national level.

Description of work

T6110 - Proposal Tool Requirement Analysis: Analysis of the requirement in terms of what will need to be developed, and what API will the program need to use from EUGAGER

T6120 - Proposal Tool Design: The general design of the program will be produced.

T6130 - Developing a standalone test case: The first test case will be produced.

T6140 - Developing the XML and API to serve data: The data generated will be released (after having been stripped of the privacy sensible data). This will happen through a specific API and a specific XML language. We shall here develop those specifications.

T6150 - Showing the tree of proposals: A graphical representation of the phylogenetic tree of proposals (which proposal gave rise the which proposal...) will be produced, permitting to the general user to understand how the process proceeded from one set of proposals to the next

T6160 - Proposal Tool Final Implementation: a final version of the program will be implemented. A version that will connect with the EUGAGER core, and through it permit to the user not just to develop the proposals, but to do it at the level of security and privacy developed of the rest of the platform

T6170 - Proposal Tool Testing and evaluation: the final version will be tested, and evaluated, in terms of speed and efficiency.

Deliverables		
Del. no.	**Deliverable name**	**Delivery (proj. month)**
D6111	Collaborative Proposal Tool Documentation	32
D6171	Collaborative Proposal Tool Standalone Test Case	9
D6172	Collaborative Proposal Tool Release v1	18
D6173	Collaborative Proposal Tool API	27
D6174	Collaborative Proposal Tool Release v2	33

Work package number	WP6200		Start date or starting event:			Month 19
Work package title	Petition Tool					
Activity type	DEM					
Participant number	1	2	3	4	5	6
Participant short name	IDEC	UNIROMA1	TFF	FCTUC	TESIA	UBO
Person-months per participant	0	0	9,5	1	0	0

Objectives

The objective is to build a toolbox application for petition creation.

Description of work

T6210 - Petition Tool Requirement Analysis: We will identify and document the requirements needed to implement a e-Petition tool that will enable users to create and sign petitions, by directly using the Tool or by using a provided API (for example, to create a Petition out of a proposal accepted by the majority of users within the Proposals Tool).

T6220 - Petition Tool Design: We will define and document the architecture and design mock-ups for the Petition tool, and its relation with the Proposals tool and the EUGAGER core.

T6230 - Petition Tool Implementation: We will implement the Petition tool as designed in the documentation previously released (D6221).

T6240 - Petition Tool API: We will design and implement an internal Application Program Interface for the Petition Tool that will enable other applications to communicate and start new petitions or sign existing petitions without forcing the user to directly use the Petition tool.

T6250 - Petition Tool Testing and Evaluation: we will run a series of

software-based tests to detect and correct bugs and we will
also select a user-group to test and evaluate the Petition tool.

Deliverables		
Del. no.	**Deliverable name**	**Delivery (proj. month)**
D6221	Petition Tool Documentation	20
D6241	Petition Tool API	24
D6251	Petition Tool Release	34

Work package number	WP6300	Start date or starting event:			Month 22	
Work package title	Toolbox Integration and Testing					
Activity type	DEM					
Participant number	1	2	3	4	5	6
Participant short name	IDEC	UNIROMA1	TFF	FCTUC	TESIA	UBO
Person-months per participant	0	0	1,25	6	4	2,5

Objectives

The objective is to test all the software developed in the previous WP, especially for what concerns their integration.

Description of work

T6310 - Trusted API Testing: we will run a series of software-based tests to detect and correct bugs about the EUGAGER APIs

T6320 - Privacy Management Testing: we will run a series of software-based tests to detect and correct bugs about the EUGAGER privacy management

T6330 - Tools Privacy Management Integration: we will run a series of software-based tests to detect and correct bugs about the toolbox applications privacy management.

T6340 - Platform Testing: We will run a series of software-based tests to detect and correct bugs and we will also select a user-group to test and evaluate the EUGAGER platform and its integration with EUGAGER tools.

Deliverables

Del. no.	Deliverable name	Delivery (proj. month)

D6311	Trusted API Testing Report	30
D6321	Privacy Management Testing Report	28
D6331	Tools Privacy Management Integration Report	31
D6341	Platform Testing Report	32

Work package number	WP6400	Start date or starting event:			Month 19	
Work package title	Collaborative Information Filtering					
Activity type	DEM					
Participant number	1	2	3	4	5	6
Participant short name	IDEC	UNIROMA1	TFF	FCTUC	TESIA	UBO
Person-months per participant	0	0	0	0	0	3,5

Objectives

The objective is to design a the collaborative recommender systems.

Description of work

T6410 - Requirement Analysis: We will describe the functionality and requirements of the collaborative recommender system.

T6420 - Design: This task involves the design of the collaborative recommender systems´ implementation..

T6430 - Implementation: This task is the implementation of all recommender functionalities.

Deliverables

Del. no.	Deliverable name	Delivery (proj. month)
D6411	Requirements Description	30
D6421	Architecture Documentation	30
D6431	Implementation Documentation	30

Work package number	WP7000	Start date or starting event:			Month 1	
Work package title	Dissemination and Exploitation					
Activity type	MGT					
Participant number	1	2	3	4	5	6
Participant short name	IDEC	UNIROMA1	TFF	FCTUC	TESIA	UBO
Person-months per participant	1	0	0	0	0	0

Objectives

- To disseminate in the communities of potential users of the EUGAGER platform and the toolbox applications.
- To increase public awareness and interest e-government applications.
- To disseminate the results to define standards.
- To prepare an exploitation plan and to implement it.

Description of work

T7100 - Publications towards the scientific community and the general public.

T7200 - Exploitation.

Deliverables

Del. no.	Deliverable name	Delivery (proj. month)
D7011	Dissemination Plan	1, 12, 24

Work package number	WP7100	Start date or starting event:			Month 1	
Work package title	Dissemination					
Activity type	MGT					
Participant number	1	2	3	4	5	6
Participant short name	IDEC	UNIROMA1	TFF	FCTUC	TESIA	UBO
Person-months per participant	5	3	2,5	0,5	1,5	3

Objectives

The objective is to promote the project by publications targeted towards the general

public and towards the scientific community.

Description of work

T7110 - Brand and Logo Design

T7120 - Project .eu Website: We will provide technical documentation to the project website. We will also manage a mailing list, a software repository and a bug tracking system open for volunteer developers in the FLOSS communities.

T7130 - Online Advertisement Campaign:

T7140 - EUGAGER Conferences (once a year): We will organize the 3 EUGAGER Conferences planned. We will present technical and non-technical sessions on the use of EUGAGER, on why Governments should build or migrate their e-participation tools on top of EUGAGER and how they can use Constituency Domains effectively, and on why the European Union should support Governments on the adoption of EUGAGER as a standard and central social networking platform for Citizen Engagement.

T7150 – University Case Studies: we will collect information from students in Partner Universities and their interest and experience with EUGAGER.

T7160 – Government Case Studies: we will collect information from Governments at all levels that are currently running e-participation/e-government sites or planning to create new ones and their interest on and eventual experience with EUGAGER

T7170 – Open Source Community Case Studies: we will collect information from other existing FLOSS communities that are currently running independent e-participation sites and their interest and experience with EUGAGER

Deliverables		
Del. no.	**Deliverable name**	**Delivery (proj. month)**
D7111	EUGAGER Logo and color palette	2
D7121	Project Website and Development Mailing List	2
D7122	Project SVN and Bug Tracking System	6
D7131	Online Campaign - Round 1	9
D7132	Online Campaign - Round 2	24
D7133	Online Campaign - Round 3	36
D7141	I EUGAGER Conference	9
D7142	II EUGAGER Conference	24
D7143	III EUGAGER Conference	36
D7151	Universities Case Study	36
D7161	Government Case Study	36
D7171	FLOSS Communities Case Study	36

Work package number	WP7200	Start date or starting event:		Month 9	
Work package title	Exploitation				
Activity type	MGT				
Participant number	1	2	3	4	5	6
Participant short name	IDEC	UNIROMA1	TFF	FCTUC	TESIA	UBO
Person-months per participant	5	1	3	4	2	0,5

Objectives

To establish and maintain contacts with potential markets and customers, to quantify the

different market segments, to determine the best techniques to penetrate the market and to

prepare for the commercial deployment of the technology and methodologies developed in the

project as well as the space science data itself.

Description of work

T7210 - Consulting Governments (at all levels) to create/migrate their Tools:

T7220 - Training Private Companies on EUGAGER Toolbox and API: We will exploit the opportunity to offer training sessions to private companies interested in learning how to create tools for EUGAGER, to be able to develop custom applications for their customers (private or public).

T7230 - Early Adoption by other FLOSS Communities: We will exploit our network of contact with current and active FLOSS Communities running independent e-participation initiatives and invite them to early adopt EUGAGER as a base platform, to join forces in reaching a critical-mass and eventually transforming it into a one-stop-shop for citizen engagement tools.

Deliverables		
Del. no.	**Deliverable name**	**Delivery (proj. month)**
D7231	Exploitation plan	18
D7232	Exploitation report	36

Table 1.3-e - Summary of Efforts

Partic. no.	Wp1	Wp2	Wp3	Wp4	Wp5	Wp6	Wp7	Tot p.m
1 IDEC	9	0	0	0	0	0	11	20
2 UNIROMA1	0	5	0	37	14	0	4	60
3 TFF	0	18	0	4	1	11,5	5,5	40
4 FCTUC	2	14	53	0,5	4	16	4,5	94
5 TESIA	0	10,5	4,5	0	0	25,5	3,5	44
6 UBO	0	13,5	30	0	7	6	3,5	60
Total	11	61	87,5	41,5	26	59,2	32	318

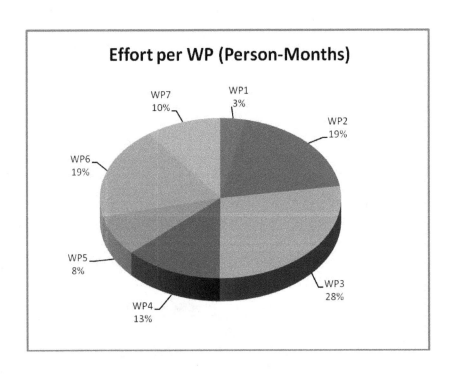

Effort per WP (Person-Months)

WP1 3%
WP2 19%
WP3 28%
WP4 13%
WP5 8%
WP6 19%
WP7 10%

Figure 10 – Effort per WP

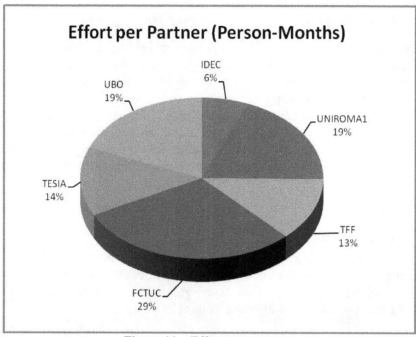

Figure 11 – Effort per partner

2   SECTION 2 - IMPLEMENTATION

2.1 Management Structure and Procedures

The successful implementation of the project has strong premises taking into consideration the pertinent project idea, the already obtained punctually results and the quality of the consortium. The management structure is built up using an effective two decision based layers, which is designed to guarantee attaining the project objectives with the given resources. This is to have on one hand an effective task-oriented management approach without having an excessively centralized schema, and to provide an appropriate management of the risk, on the other hand.

The first decision layer is promoted by the partners involved in the specific tasks, who are clustered around the WPs leaders. Basically, each WPs leader is responsible for the achievement of the specific outcomes. The effective clusters of participants are already defined being reflected into WPs descriptions (Tab.1.3c) and into the Summary staff effort (Tab.1.3d). This layer guarantees a parallel operative structure providing the effective control of progress and results in the specific WPs.

The second decision layer holds the leaders of the WPs into a Project Steering Committee (PSO) under the control of the Project Coordinator (PCO) who perform an effective control of progress and results of the project. PCO will perform the assessment of progress and results according to the defined milestones and deliverables. The PCO will be also the Project Manager (PM).

The first workpackage (WP1) is the work block devoted to the Project Management including specific management activities over the whole duration of the project. This key work package includes essential components, detailed as follows:

1.0.0.0. Project Management and Coordination
        1.0.1.0. Ensure technical and contractual interface with EU
        1.0.2.0. Provide guidelines to partners, for the execution of their activities in accordance with EU guidelines, and control performance and progress.
        1.0.3.0. Preparation of inputs for project reviews according to the EU Call

1.0.4.0. Report project progress and status to EU.

1.0.5.0. Identify events which could affect the achievement of the project objectives, and plan recovery actions.

1.0.6.0. Scheduling, reporting and train - Its support staff to meet all EU requirements

1.1.0.0.   Consortium Management

Overall coordination:

1.1.1.0. Ensure that resources (manpower/material, etc.) are available for the successful performance of the project.

1.1.2.0. Evaluation of project performance, identification of deficiencies/inadequacies, and implementation of corrective actions; control project progress.

1.1.3.0. Identify events which could affect the achievement of the project objectives, and plan recovery actions.

1.1.4.0. Interface and manage information flow among all the project Tasks

1.1.5.0. Ensure the timeliness of all the deliverables.

Contract and Financial Management:

1.1.6.0. Monitor the Annual Cost Statements

1.1.7.0. Attendance in team meetings monitoring the compliance with contractual conditions

1.1.8.0. Advise project manager on contractual status and implications

1.1.9.0. Initialise invoicing and payment on request or approval of the project manager

1.2.0.0.   Assessment of Progress and Results

1.2.1.0. Preparation of inputs for project reviews according to the EU Call

1.2.2.0. Perform and document project meetings with project team

1.2.3.0. Documentation Management

1.2.4.0. Establishment of documentation and document control guidelines and procedures

Some management components in the project are sharable among the participants, but others are not. At the same time, the financial issue is one of the most important instruments of management. In order to guarantee tangible results on the proposed objectives of the project, this component will be exclusively directed by the PCO. Special attention will be paid to the financial reporting in correlation with the deliverables in the project.

In the following section we describe in detail how the management effort supports the rolling of the project. Several procedures included in the specific plans were derived in order to deal with the complexity and scale of the project, as follows:

Plan for knowledge management

Resources planning

Contingency planning

Knowledge is one of the most important resources in the project. In the beginning it plays the role of the "seed" including the project idea, the objectives and the proposed ways to reach them. The knowledge is the resource that guides the other resources required in the project: financial, material and human. As a matter of fact, the plan for knowledge management has a close interdependency with the additional plans. Considering communication as the key issue of the knowledge management we have a clear approach on the instruments and practices to be used. A specific human resource of the PCO is designed to undertake this work. The proposed generic structure for knowledge management plan is presented in the following table.

Nr. Crt.	Type of appointment/mean of communication	Participants involved	Date/Period and place
	Meeting Videoconference Seminar/Workshop Regular e-mail/ internet chat/web log	All partners	(Scheduled or extraordinary)
Practices	**Activities on time table and chairing**		**Status**
To identify Knowledge To create Knowledge To represent Knowledge To distribute knowledge	- Sharing of points of view; IP (intellectual property) identification; Documents draw up/drafting; Results Validation; Dissemination		Done Postponed Cancelled

The Plan will follow the rolling of the project providing an effective track record of the partners. It also facilitates sensing the risk in the early stages and making the appropriate decision for management of the contingency. The Plan of knowledge management provides mandatory appointments before deliverable are expected and at the milestones. The conclusions of the appointments will be registered and will be part of the track records of the partners, becoming a basis for current decisions.

At the beginning of the project, PCO will schedule the starting reunion with a large group of the staff from each partner involved in the project. This happened two weeks after the starting date at PCO headquarters. The starting reunion agenda is focused on the project implementation plan including technical aspects and financial issues. A special point of the starting reunion is dedicated to the appointment of the members in Project Steering Committee (PSC) including the responsible persons for intellectual property and the financial consultant. This starting reunion also contributes to the better mutual acquaintance among the partners. The current meetings

are planned to take place cyclically at the partners headquarter. In fact, the flexibility of the work is provided by the independence of the activities in the WPs that are clearly defined in order to avoid the cross-interactions on their progress. The members of PSC assemble in current reunions and/or in extraordinary meetings. The current reunions are scheduled according to the project's milestones, while the extraordinary meetings take place when possible special issues arise (for example, for risk analysis).

Communications procedure between the partners is the subject of the Knowledge management plan. This will be mainly based on the electronic mail for official document exchange. The phone will be used exceptionally for current arrangements and explanations. The official language is English.

As it concerns the management of the resources, each participant organization is in charge of the local resource management under the control of its coordinator. A large part of resources is human because the project implies a huge R&D effort as well as a tremendous management effort. As all the partners are currently working in the area of R&D they provide the best practices for time management to mobilize the human resources towards reaching the successfully objectives.

Material resources are involved directly in R&D activities. Some of the tasks are strongly dependent on the equipment and special components/devices that will be subject to supply management. At this moment we know what equipments we need but the consortium should decide on the technology. In three months from the starting date PSO will have clear enough vision about the technology to be involved in the project. Certain Data Sheets (material specifications) for supply and material acquisitions with EU contribution will be drawn up.

Other resources required in the project, like telecommunication services (data transfer) strictly used for testing and demonstration activities in the project, will be the subject of contractual and financial management according to the acquisition regulations in each country.

More details about the resources to be committed in the project are given in Sub section 2.4.

2.2 Individual Participants

For each participant in the proposed project, provide a brief description of the legal entity, the main tasks they have been attributed, and the previous experience relevant to those tasks. Provide also a short profile of the individuals who will be undertaking the work.

2.2.1 IDEC

Role of IDEC. In EUGAGER project IDEC will be leading the management and the coordination of the consortium (WP1) and will also be responsible for the dissemination and exploitation of the project and its results (WP7).

About IDEC. IDEC is a training and consultancy company based in Piraeus, Greece. Clients of IDEC are both SMEs and the larger Greek companies, Entrepreneurs' Associations, Universities and Chambers of Commerce/Industry. The personnel are mainly mechanical, electrical and software engineers with post-graduate studies and long-term industrial experience.

The main areas of activities are training and management consulting, ISO-9001, software and multimedia development, internet applications, distance learning, e-business, e-commerce, telecommunications and networks.

Relevant Background. IDEC has long experience in participation in European projects. Such projects that demonstrate IDEC's previous experience in the field of ICT are: (1)*e-Living- Life in a Digital Europe:* Large-scale comparative panel study for the description and explanation of the behaviour relating to the uptake and usage of information and communications technology (ICT) at the domestic level. (2)*EduCAT-* Education Content Assembly Tool: Testbed of a new, innovative, multimedia toolset by educators who will evaluate the functionality, acceptability and usability of the toolset by using it to produce interactive education software. (3)*WebSET* (Web-based Standard Education Tools) - Development of advanced Web-based technologies to implement innovative cost-effective learning tools.

Also, IDEC with its technical and training capacities supports the activities of various social structures like the Psychological Centre of North Greece, the Psychiatric Hospital of Thessaloniki, the National Organisation of Social Care, the Federation of Volunteer non profit organisation of Greece, the Society of Psychiatric Health and Sanity, the centre of Art Therapy, the General Regional Hospital of Volos etc.

Key personnel. Sofia Spiliotopoulou: Graduate of the National Technical University of Athens with a Degree in Chemical engineering and from University of Athens with a degree in Economics. She also has a MSc degree in Regional development. She started her career in 1983 as SMEs consultant in EOMMEX (Hellenic Organisation for the promotion of SMEs) and she has been the Director of Education Department from 1984 to 1990 and Director of EU projects from 1990 to 1995. Since 1991 she is the cofounder of IDEC SA. She speaks fluently Greek, English, French, very good Italian and good German and Spanish.

Panos Katsambanis: He is a Mechanical and Electrical Engineer, graduate of the National Technical University of Athens and holds a M.Sc. in Regional Development. He has more than 25 years experience as a consultant and trainer at seminars organised for businessmen and supervisors in the topics: management, economics, production planning and control, cost control, logistics, quality management systems, multimedia and software development. He is the cofounder of IDEC SA. He speaks fluently Greek and English.

Natassa Kazantzidou: She is a graduate from the faculty of Chemical Engineers of the National Technical University of Athens (1995). Since 1999 she works at IDEC SA, with main responsibilities business consulting and management of European projects in the field of VET. She has experience in SMEs management and development, vocational training, multimedia and internet applications. She is computer skilled and speaks Greek, English, Spanish and French.

Xenia Chronopoulou: Graduate of the Business Administration and Economics department of the University of Piraeus. She holds a MSc in Computer Science from the University College London, UK. She is a certified ISO 9001:2000 auditor from IRCA. Since 2003 she is working for IDEC S.A. in the field of European Projects, with particular experience in the field of quality assurance, ICT and vocational training. She speaks Greek, English, French and Spanish.

George Velegrakis: He is an Electrical and Computer Engineer, graduate of the National Technical University of Athens. He holds a M.Sc. in Environmental Policies and Development. Since 2008 he works for IDEC as project manager. He speaks fluently Greek, English and German.

2.2.2 Sapienza University of Rome

Role of UNIROMA1. In this project UNIROMA1 contribution will mainly focus on security and transparency issues by designing protocols to satisfy such conflicting requirements and by formally verifying by model checking the correctness of the novel proposed protocols.

About UNIROMA1. The Computer Science Department (http://www.dsi.uniroma1.it) of the Sapienza University of Rome currently has about 40 faculties, 20 Ph.D Students and 5 Post-Docs. All main Computer Science research areas are represented. Typically each faculty is active in one or more research areas. This creates informal research groups (Labs) on many research themes. Examples are: Algorithms, Computer Networks, Human Computer Interaction, Information Retrieval, Model Checking, Security, Software Engineering, Web Semantics. The research groups involved in this project are the *Information and Communication Security* (ICS) group (http://icsecurity.di.uniroma1.it) and the *Model Checking* (MC) group.

Relevant Background. The ICS research group activity includes: applied cryptography; key management, authentication, confidentiality, privacy & anonymity, intrusion detection and prevention, Web application security, access Control, trust management, vulnerability assessment and exploit analysis.

The MC research group activity includes: algorithm and tools for the automatic verification via model checking of concurrent, stochastic as well as hybrid systems; protocol verification; automatic synthesis of reactive systems (controllers as well as supervisory controllers) from formal specifications.

As part of our research activities the following *research software* has been implemented and released as open source software. **WHIPS** (*Windows Host Intrusion Prevention System-http://whips.sourceforge.net/*) is a prototype software for monitoring critical system calls which may be used to subvert the execution of privileged Windows applications. **REMUS** (*REference Monitor for Unix Systems - http://remus.sourceforge.net/*) is a prototype system for monitoring critical system calls which may be used to subvert the execution of privileged Unix applications. **BSP** is an OBDD based model checker for automatic synthesis of reactive C programs (*controllers*) from finite state DESs (*Discrete Even Systems*) plant models and formal specifications for the closed loop system. **CMurphi** (*Caching Murphi*) is a disk based extension of the Stanford University verifier Murphi. CMurphi has been widely used at INTEL for verification of Cache Coherence Protocol. **FHP-Murphi** (*Finite Horizon Probabilistic Murphi*) is an explicit disk based bounded model checker for discrete time stochastic processes. **HSMV** is a SAT based bounded model checker for Discrete Time Piecewise Affine Hybrid Systems. **NashMV**, is a model checker for *Multi Administrative Domain* (MAD) Distributed Systems (i.e. distributed systems where each node owns its resources and there is no central authority owning all system nodes) designed in collaboration with the CS Department of the Univ. of Texas at Austin (USA).

The research groups ICS and MC are regularly involved in many national as well as international research projects sponsored by: the EC (European Community), ESA (European Space Agency), CNR (National Council of Research), ENEA (National Institute for

Alternative Energies), MIUR (Italian Ministry for University and Research) as well as private industries. Here is a selected list of some of them. **SSFRT** (*System and Software Functional Requirements Techniques*, ESA); **ULISSE** (*USOCs KnowLedge Integration and Dissemination for Space Science Experimentation,* EC FP7**), EYES** (*Energy Efficient Sensor Networks*, EC), **SAPP** (*Advanced System for Fault Tolerant Design of Wireless Networks,* MIUR:*), **INTERCEPTOR** (*Motion Planning with moving obstacles,* Industrial project funded by INTECS**), TRAMP** (*An Integrated Control and Management System for the Safe Transport of Dangerous Goods,* MIUR:), **WEBMINDS** (MIUR). **SETRAM** (*A Logistic Expert System for the Optimisation of Multimodal Freight Transportation,* ENEA).

Key personnel. Luigi V. Mancini. Prof. Mancini (http://www.di.uniroma1.it/mancini) received the PhD degree in Computer Science from the University of Newcastle upon Tyne, UK, in 1989, and the Laurea degree in Computer Science from the University of Pisa, Italy, in 1983. From 2000, he is a full professor of Computer Science at the Dipartimento di Informatica of the Sapienza University of Rome. Since 1994, he is a visiting research professor of the Center for Secure Information Systems, GMU, Virginia, USA. His current research interests include: computer network and information security, secure multicast communication, public key infrastructure, authentication protocols, system survivability, computer privacy, wireless network security, fault-tolerant distributed systems, and large-scale peer-to-peer systems. He published more than 70 scientific papers in international conferences and journals. He served in the program committees of several international conferences such as: ACM Conference on Computer and Communication Security, ACM Conference on Conceptual Modeling, ACM Symposium on Access Control Models and Technology, ACM Workshop of Security of Ad-hoc and Sensor Networks, IEEE Securecomm.

Luigi Mancini was the founder of Information and Communication Security (ICSecurity) Laboratory. Currently he is a member of the Scientific Board of the Italian Communication Police force, the director of the Master degree programs in Information and Network Security of the Sapienza University of Rome. He was the supervisor of the Italian team that won the International Java Platform Programming Contest 2006 awarded in San Francisco, USA.

Enrico   Tronci.   Since   2001   Enrico   Tronci (http://www.dsi.uniroma1.it/~tronci) is an Associate Professor with the Computer Science Department of the Sapienza University of Rome (Italy). From 1994 to 2000 he has been a Researcher with the Computer Science Department of the University of L'Aquila (Italy). From 1992 to 1993 he has been a Post-Doct at LIP (Laboratoire pour l'Informatique du Parallelisme) at the ENS (Ecole Normal Superior) of Lyon (France). In 1991, under the supervision of Prof. Richard Statman, he received his Ph.D degree from Carnegie Mellon University, Pittsburgh, USA. In 1987, under the supervision of Prof. Corrado Boehm and Prof. Giorgio Ausiello, he received his Master degree in Electrical Engineering from the Sapienza University of Rome. His Master Thesis received the IBM-Italia prize for the best Master Thesis in Artificial Intelligence. His current research interests comprise: Automatic verification of safety and security properties of concurrent systems, Model checking algorithms, Hybrid systems, Automatic synthesis of reactive programs. He authored more than 50 scientific papers on international journals and conferences. He has been Conference Chair for the CHARME (Correct Hardware Design and Verification methods) conference and in the program committee of conferences such as: FMCAD (Formal Methods in Computer Aided Design), CHARME, FDL. Enrico Tronci participates as principal investigator to many research projects sponsored by the European Community, ESA, CNR, ENEA, MIUR as well as from private industries.

2.2.3   Associazione Telematics Freedom Foundation

Role of TFF. The Telematics Freedom Foundation will work developing the Web Interface for the EUGAGER Toolbox, using the primitives and API's developed by other partners previously in the project. TFF will participate in requirement analysis, architecture definition and design for the Toolbox platform and will lead the work for the Petition Tool. TFF will also use its expertise to support other partners in tasks regarding Privacy Access Controls, Identity Management and Web Application Security. TFF will contribute to Dissemination and Exploitation activities and will use its contact network to engage existing e-participation/e-democracy FLOSS communities in the project by using EUGAGER and giving feedback while in execution phase.

About TFF. The Telematics Freedom Foundation was created to bring in the age of telematics, Internet, mobile phones and the web, all those freedoms and rights that the Free Software Movement has already brought to PC users worldwide. To achieve this purpose, we promote the consolidation and widespread adoption of models for development and deployment of telematic services which are under the full control of their users.

Our general goal is the furthering of democracy, including media and global democracy, through the promotion of telematic solutions that enable the protection and extension of the communication and participation rights of all people. We believe the development of such tools and their wide adoption to be a crucial element in sustaining "by example" a broader political movement for the affirmation of those rights in public institutions and legislations at all levels.

Relevant Background. TFF runs a series of projects aimed at promoting media and global democracy through the use of telematic services that can be full controlled by the users.

Media Democracy. Popolobue.TV is a webTV channel featuring socio-political and satirical content, completely controlled by its viewers: from production to post-production, publishing, advertising and distribution; The Freedom Box Project promotes the wide dissemination and standardization of TV Media Centers connected to the web that are easy to use and economic for anyone; and by anyone verifiable and customizable; The Social Video Packs Project aims to create and maintain physical labs open to all citizens and equipped for creation, editing and post-production of "Social Video" and tutoring on "Citizen Journalism" around media freedom and democracy, based on two models of Social Media tested successfully in Brazil: the "Pontos de Cultura" and "Estúdio Livre".

Global Democracy. Continuous Democracy is a project aiming to collect efforts and promote a series of software tools, methodologies and telematics infrastructures focused on security, reliability and scalability to support the growing number of people interested in Public Activism: Draft2Gether, a collaborative text feedback tool, allowing groups of 8-100 people to participate in commenting on and amending documents to rapidly reach consensus. Users can quickly vote and automatically approve/reject text amendments; Rule2Gether: a general-purpose consensus-building and decision-making tool, to organize agenda items and proposals within any organization willing to empower its members by collecting their feedback; Decide2Gether: an add-on module providing Functionality and User Interface for online preference expression; Do2Gether: a political social networking and groups management application.

Key personnel. Rufo Guerreschi - Founder and CEO

Rufo completed his education through graduate programs in public affairs and IT at Princeton and Rutgers Universities (1998-1999). He has held (1999-2001) executive technical and commercial positions at advanced server-side software providers, such as 4thpass in New York and Urban Data Solutions in Seattle, USA. While there, he managed web-application projects and then led the world-wide pre-sale, sale and technical deployment of multi-million dollar web-based software solutions for global mobile operators such as Vodafone, Telefonica, DoCoMo, etc.

He founded and managed ParTecs - Participatory Technologies (2002-2007), a company which deployed social networking telematics systems based on free and open source software over three continents, with research and development facilities in Pune and Bangalore, India. As CEO of Tecnoconsult International, a group of real estate development companies controlled by his family, he is leading a project for a multifunctional complex of 60-100,000 square meters centred on audiovisual media, internationalization, ICT and innovation, located 5 minutes from Rome.

Being a longstanding international political activist in the field of global democratization, he worked for several NGOs in the area and later founded the Telematics Freedom Foundation, based in Rome.

Giovani Spagnolo - Program Director. Giovani Spagnolo graduated in Computer Science from the Pontifícia Universidade Católica do Rio Grande do Sul (PUCRS) in Porto Alegre - Brazil, with an Executive MBA in Strategic Enterprise Management from the University of São Paulo (USP). He wrote several articles on ICT/Free Software for the Entrepreneurs Academy Portal, and he is one of the founders and activists behind the Free Software movement in Brazil, and member of the organizing committee of Latin America's biggest Forum on Free Software (FISL), held annually in Porto Alegre.

Giovani started his career back in 1998, in Porto Alegre, working for PROCERGS, the data processing company for the state of Rio Grande do Sul. With solid experience in planning and analysis of web projects, he later founded his own Free Software company called WebYES! Internet Systems and later moved to Rome to coordinate a Digital Inclusion project promoted by the Digital Youth Consortium and the Municipality of Rome. Since 2004 he works with planning and user interface for e-Participation and e-Democracy web based applications. Since 2007 he is the Program Director for the Telematics Freedom Foundation.

2.2.4 Universidade de Coimbra

Role of FCTUC. FCTUC will work on the creation, learning, and tracking of knowledge in the e-government website. They will develop the Folksonomy system which will permit to track the knowledge generated by the system. As well as develop the algorithm that will create new knowledge, by letting the users produce and explore the space of possible proposals (to be brought up to the policy makers), and evaluate each other proposals.

About FCTUC. Faculty of Sciences and Technology is the major faculty within the University of Coimbra, an indisputable reference in higher education and research in Portugal, due to the quality of the courses taught and to the advances achieved in pure and applied research in various areas of knowledge. The FCTUC holds 14 Departments, that cover the majority of the scientific areas of the Natural, Physical, and Exact Sciences, of Engineering, of Life, of Architecture and of Anthropology and, as enclosed establishments, the Museums of Natural History and of Physics, the Botanical Garden, the Geophysical Institute and the Astrononomy Observatory. FCTUC offers to its students, around 7000, a wide and comprehensive group of graduate and postgraduate courses, master´s degrees, and doctorate programs, as well as specific life-long training programs, with a teaching staff of about 500, whose high quality is widely recognized, developing their research activities in 20 integrated FCT Research Units and several Associated Research Units that constitute a national and international reference in the production of science in a vast number of fields. FCTUC explores also its scientific potential in the transfer of knowledge and to the development of businesses and industry, through the Pedro Nunes Institute (IPN), a well succeeded pioneer structure whose services are used within the scope of entrepreneurial incubation and entrepreneurship.

Relevant Background. The Evolutionary and Complex Systems Group is specialised in Genetic Algorithm and Genetic programming, which is be at the base of the Group Knowledge Creation process. In fact the knowledge creation process will be at its core a genetic algorithm that uses human beings to produce viable mutations of existing proposals, as well as to evaluate them. The P.I. for the project has more than 10 years of experience in modelling and studying evolutionary systems, and producing systems with evolutionary behaviour.

Key personnel. Pietro Speroni di Fenizio (P.I.): Dr. Pietro Speroni di Fenizio is a Research Assistent at the Evolutionary and Complex Systems Group, which is part of the - Centre for Informatics and Systems of the University of Coimbra (CISUC), Departamento de Engenharia Informática; Faculdade Ciencias e Tecnologia; Universidade de Coimbra. In his academic activity Dr Speroni has specialised in using mathematical models to study natural systems. His interests range from Theoretical Biology to e-government, to Web2.0. His PhD was focused on developing and clearly defining mathematically a new theory to study novelty in chemical system (Chemical Organisation Theory). His main passion is the study of evolutionary system, and the reproduction of artificial system with equivalent novel generative power. He has a long standing blog; there, in Summer 2005 (http://blog.pietrosperoni.it/cat/publishable/) he was the first to suggest that tags could be used to impose a metric between the tagged resources (in that case web pages). In that occasion he also suggested how, since the weighted list of tags represent the culture of the people that tagged those resources, they can be used to track changes in the culture. Those results were later expanded, and developed by other groups.

He has a long interest in the e-government, and in general in the form that should take democracy in the 21st Century. Two of his talks (one on tags, and one on e-government) are available online at http://videolectures.net/pietro_speroni_di_fenizio/. His publications are available at: http://publications.pietrosperoni.it/.

2.2.5 TESIA

Role of TESIA. Turnfont Ecological Social Internet Activism (TESIA) will work on three main areas. Firstly, TESIA will implement a broad folksonomy system in the Platform core. Secondly, TESIA will participate in the development of a Stand Alone Test Case (as a research prototype) of the Collaborative Proposal Tool. Thirdly, TESIA will participate in the development of, and fully implement, the Collaborative Proposal Tool.

About TESIA. Turnfront (TESIA) is social-mission company formed to assist charitable and online democracy projects, through the use of web technologies. Our goals include increasing citizen participation in democratic and decision-making processes. We have been involved in projects gathering information and opinions, organising these to allow broad participation, and refactoring them into easily-digestable summaries.

Key personnel. Chris Anderson - Turnfront Director

Chris graduated in Artificial Intelligence at the University of Sussex. He went on to project manage the redevelopment of a series of large charity websites, before forming Turnfront. Since then, he has project managed several large web projects, implementing them using Open Source Content Management Systems. He has also participated in wiki projects using deliberative structures to facilitate group policy writing.

He has worked in the offices of a Member of the UK Parliament, presented to senior Government politicians on using online democracy systems, and worked with charities on political lobbying.

2.2.6 University of Bonn

Role of UBO. The main task of UBO to EUGAGER is the deployment of information retrieval techniques, collaborative information filtering in particular, to support the users (citizens and policy makers alike) and to provide additional value to them. New challenges are posed by the EUGAGER toolbox and the applications, necessitating additional research in the field of information retrieval and filtering.

About UBO. The Institute of Computer Science, University of Bonn, is a scientific institution of the Faculty of Mathematics and Natural Science of the *Rheinische Friedrich-Wilhelms Universität Bonn*. It comprises of six departments with 16 professors and more than 100 staff members.

The department *Institut für Informatik III* (practical and applied computer science) is headed by Prof. Dr. Armin B. Cremers and has currently 38 employees, including 5 professors and 26 researchers. The research fields are, among others, in the areas of scientific databases, information retrieval and digital libraries, internet information systems, software engineering, computer security, artificial intelligence, autonomous mobile systems, intelligent vision systems, multi-media retrieval, pattern recognition, descriptive programming, and foundations and applications of knowledge-based systems.

Relevant Background. The long-time research in information retrieval covers multiple fields including information retrieval in structured documents (SGML/XML), natural language interfaces, peer-to-peer and social information retrieval. The research of the information retrieval group is currently focussed on collaborative approaches which are based on social interaction. Especially the concept of Virtual Knowledge Communities and the combination of personalisation, collaboration and social interaction in web communities are being explored. Part of this work has been done in cooperation with Prof. Dr. Douglas W. Oard, University of Maryland.

Our experience in social information retrieval has also been applied to interdisciplinary research and applications, for example in joint projects with the German Reference Centre for Ethics in the Life Sciences (DRZE), founded on 1 January, 1999. DRZE is a national documentation and information centre for the entire field of ethics in biomedical and life sciences. It was founded with the mission to scientifically provide the foundations for a qualified bioethical discussion within a German, European as well as an international framework. Prof. Dr. Armin B. Cremers is a member of the supervisory board of DRZE.

Another part of our research activities are internet information systems. We have been working on data models for content management systems (CMS), application of XML technologies to CMS, query optimisation in XML databases and combining distributed web content management with desktop publishing.

Our group looks back at nearly two decades of research in computer security. Topics include database and operating system security as well as software security m*etrics* for malware resilience.

Key personnel. Prof. Dr. Armin B. Cremers is the director of the department *Institut für Informatik III* in the institute of Computer Science at the University of Bonn science since 1990.

Dr. Stefan Lüttringhaus-Kappel is a senior scientific assistant at the *Institut für Informatik III*. He received his diploma in computer science from Dortmund University in 1987 and his doctoral degree in computer science from Bonn University in 1992, working in on theory and applications of logic programming. His current areas of work are internet information systems and XML technologies.

Tobias Rudorf is a researcher and Ph.D. student at the *Institut für Informatik III*. He received his diploma in Computer Science from Bonn University in 2007. His field of research is information retrieval.

2.3   Consortium as a Whole

In the following we describe why the consortium is credible and capable of coping with the objectives of the project.

First, the strength of the consortium was experienced during the period of proposal preparation. Initially, the Coordinator had to select participants from those who expressed the interest for the project. They had the possibility to know about the project idea from different sources.

An important role in partner searching had TFF (p3) which provided a refined list with relevant participants. The consortium is highly motivated by the idea of this project because it is matched with their expertise and own interest in developing.

Despite the fact that the consortium does not look like the traditional STREP consortia regarding the number of participants, we are confident because of the critical mass for a "programme approach" have been mobilized. Based on the each partner's potential (human, experience, equipment and finance) the consortium has the optimum size that covers the typical activities of a STREP: research and innovation, demonstration, training, and management.

The purpose is to create a "virtual place" where citizens across Europe can meet to exchange their ideas and express them, and to assure them that their administrators will take care of their opinions. Thinking about the great success achieved today by social networks, we think that this approach could be applied to e-government to attain the same engagement by the citizens.

This will have some important impacts both on citizen's life and on the governance of Member States of the European Union, but also on scientific research and on European position on the industry of cooperative platforms.

The consortium has an appropriate pan-European representation: Italy, Portugal, Greece, Germany and the United Kingdom. The consortium is also well-balanced regarding its specific composition, grouping by activities type the following: 3 (three) Universities, 1(one) Research centres/Institutes, 2 (two) SMEs.

The consortium has a complementary structure that guarantees performing the specific tasks and to achieve the project complex objectives in a coherent way. In the following table is presented the summary of attribution, experience and competencies of the participants that is relevant for the project implementation describing.

Partner Short Name	Attributions	Competencies	Experience
IDEC	• Coordination of the project and the consortium • Coordination of dissemination and exploitation activities	Training and management consulting; Long experience in participation and in coordination in (European) projects	e-Living- Life in a Digital Europe: Large-scale comparative panel study for the description and explanation of the behaviour relating to the uptake and usage of information and communications technology (ICT) at the domestic level. EduCAT- Education Content Assembly Tool: Testbed of a new, innovative, multimedia toolset by educators who will evaluate the functionality, acceptability and usability of the toolset by using it to produce interactive education software. WebSET (Web-based Standard Education Tools) - Development of advanced Web-based technologies to implement innovative cost-effective learning tools.
UNIROMA1	• Security and transparency issues	Research in Algorithms, Computer Networks, Human Computer Interaction, Information Retrieval, Model	WHIPS (Windows Host Intrusion Prevention System- http://whips.sourceforge.net/) is a prototype software for monitoring critical system calls which may be used to subvert the execution of

Partner Short Name	Attributions	Competencies	Experience
		Checking, Security, Software Engineering, Web Semantics	privileged Windows applications.
			REMUS (REference Monitor for Unix Systems - http://remus.sourceforge.net/) is a prototype system for monitoring critical system calls which may be used to subvert the execution of privileged Unix applications.
			BSP is an OBDD based model checker for automatic synthesis of reactive C programs (controllers) from finite state DESs (Discrete Even Systems) plant models and formal specifications for the closed loop system.
			CMurphi (Caching Murphi) is a disk based extension of the Stanford University verifier Murphi. CMurphi has been widely used at INTEL for verification of Cache Coherence Protocol.
			FHP-Murphi (Finite Horizon Probabilistic Murphi) is an explicit disk based bounded model checker for discrete time stochastic processes.
			HSMV is a SAT based bounded model checker for Discrete Time Piecewise Affine Hybrid Systems.

Partner Short Name	Attributions	Competencies	Experience
			NashMV, is a model checker for Multi Administrative Domain (MAD) Distributed Systems (i.e. distributed systems where each node owns its resources and there is no central authority owning all system nodes) designed in collaboration with the CS Department of the Univ. of Texas at Austin (USA).
TFF	<ul><li>Requirement analysis</li><li>Architecture definition</li><li>Design for the Toolbox platform</li><li>Work for the Petition Tool</li><li>Privacy Access Controls</li><li>Identity Management</li><li>Web Application</li></ul>	Promotion of the consolidation and widespread adoption of models for development and deployment of telematic services which are under the full control of their users	Media Democracy. Popolobue.TV is a webTV channel featuring socio-political and satirical content, completely controlled by its viewers: from production to post-production, publishing, advertising and distribution; The Freedom Box Project promotes the wide dissemination and standardization of TV Media Centers connected to the web that are easy to use and economic for anyone; and by anyone verifiable and customizable; The Social Video Packs Project aims to create and maintain physical labs open to all citizens and equipped for creation, editing and post-production of "Social Video" and tutoring on "Citizen Journalism" around media freedom and democracy,

Partner Short Name	Attributions	Competencies	Experience
	Security		based on two models of Social Media tested successfully in Brazil: the "Pontos de Cultura" and "Estúdio Livre". Global Democracy. Continuous Democracy is a project aiming to collect efforts and promote a series of software tools, methodologies and telematics infrastructures focused on security, reliability and scalability to support the growing number of people interested in Public Activism: Draft2Gether, a collaborative text feedback tool, allowing groups of 8-100 people to participate in commenting on and amending documents to rapidly reach consensus. Users can quickly vote and automatically approve/reject text amendments; Rule2Gether: a general-purpose consensus-building and decision-making tool, to organize agenda items and proposals within any organization willing to empower its members by collecting their feedback; Decide2Gether: an add-on module providing Functionality and User Interface for online preference expression; Do2Gether: a political social networking and groups management application.

Partner Short Name	Attributions	Competencies	Experience
FCTUC	• Creation, learning • Tracking of knowledge in the e-government website.	Specialised in: Genetic Algorithm and Genetic programming (Group Knowledge Creation process).	More than 10 years of experience in modelling and studying evolutionary systems, and producing systems with evolutionary behaviour.
TESIA	• Implement a broad folksonomy system in the Platform core • Participation in the development of a Stand Alone Test Case (as a research prototype) of the Collaborative Proposal Tool. • Participation in	Social-mission company formed to assist charitable and online democracy projects, through the use of web technologies.	Involvement in projects gathering information and opinions, organising these to allow broad participation, and refactoring them into easily-digestable summaries.

Partner Short Name	Attributions	Competencies	Experience
	the development of, and fully implement, the Collaborative Proposal Tool.		

Partner Short Name	Attributions	Competencies	Experience
UBO	• Deployment of information retrieval techniques, collaborative information filtering in particular, to support the users (citizens and policy makers alike) and to provide additional value to them.	Research fields (among others) in the areas of: scientific databases, information retrieval and digital libraries, internet information systems, software engineering, computer security, artificial intelligence, autonomous mobile systems, intelligent vision systems, multi-media retrieval, pattern recognition, descriptive programming, and foundations and applications of knowledge-based systems.	Internet information systems. Work on data models for content management systems (CMS), application of XML technologies to CMS, query optimisation in XML databases and combining distributed web content management with desktop publishing. The group looks back at nearly two decades of research in computer security. Topics include database and operating system security as well as software security metrics for malware resilience.

2.4 Resources to Be Committed

Additionally to the huge human effort in the project an important part of costs is allocated for the equipment. The project benefits by the complementary resources to the EC contribution. Moreover than their own experience (reflected by human resources), each partner has to mobilize a part of their current infrastructure, (material resources and services) that will contribute to the progress of the project. In fact, this aspect was one of the points that had awarded them the quality of partner in this project.

The overall financial plan for the project is credible tailored to the resources that will be integrated in the project. Basically the personnel cost was estimated taking in to consideration the daily rate ceilings in each country of participant and the average number of full time person month involved. Possibly co-financing (from the own funds) of the personnel cost if need as well as partially covering of the auxiliary personnel cost from the indirect costs are pertinent solutions. The cost for material resources is built on the technical specifications of the required equipment and software specifications. Other component of the costs results in the context of demonstration activities and other activities including the cost of specific services for testing, certifications, telecommunications.

3 SECTION 3 - IMPACT

3.1 *Expected impacts listed in the work programme*

The purpose of the EUGAGER project is to design and implement a secure, transparent and knowledge-based platform for e-government and e-participation, combining security, knowledge creation, sharing and tracking, extensibility and scalability.

The purpose is to create a "virtual place" where citizens across Europe can meet to exchange their ideas and express them, and to assure them that their administrators will take care of their opinions. Thinking about the great success achieved today by social networks, we think that this approach could be applied to e-government to attain the same engagement by the citizens.

This will have some important impacts both on citizen's life and on the governance of Member States of the European Union, but also on scientific research and on European position on the industry of cooperative platforms.

In the following paragraphs, all these aspects will be broadly described, to show how this project could lead to a positive impact on our society. In particular, we will show how the expected impacts listed in the work programme will be addressed (par. 3.1.1), which are the assumptions and external factors which could affect the expected impacts (par. 3.1.2), why this project requires a European approach (3.1.4) and, finally, which are the related projects, concerning the research fields of interest for EUGAGER (par. 3.1.4).

3.1.1 Contribution to the Expected Impacts listed in the work programme

> *"Improved empowerment and engagement of individuals, groups and communities in policy making processes"*

EUGAGER will provide a way to unify European citizens around the public activism in a social ecosystem of tools aimed at e-participation and e-governance. To achieve this result, the dissemination phase of the project will assume a fundamental importance.

EUGAGER will contribute to enhance the engagement of individuals, group and communities in policy making process by the following activities:

-   Receiving support from governments (at all levels), which will stimulate citizens to participate to the policy-making process.
-   Disseminating the Project goal within existing FLOSS communities. The early engagement of FLOSS Communities that currently run independent e-participation sites is crucial to create a sustainable development community around the EUGAGER Core.

-   Allowing the distinction of "secure" and "non-secure" authentication procedures. Thus users will be encouraged to use the EUGAGER tools, as they will be able to choose if they want to identify themselves or just to use the services provided as a non verified user. This will hopefully enlarge the user base and replicate the viral effect inherent of Web2.0 applications to engage more and more users.
-   Organising specific press events and communicating with journalists to ensure publications in journals and magazines papers with a large distribution.

EUGAGER will contribute to enhance the empowerment of individuals, group and communities in policy making process by:

-   Assuring users the transparency of the policy-making activities and giving them the possibility to check and verify the toolbox's data and processes;
-   Allowing users to express their preferences, and assuring that they will be taken into account by governors throughout an entire transparent process.

The objective of all that is to put together the best European expertise in order to promote the mobilization of the widest possible community of users around the European utilization of the EUGAGER platform.

> *"Increased trust of the citizens through transparency and feedback of their contributions and more efficient collection of feedback"*

One of the major challenges for e-Government frameworks is to assure transparency, that is to give to the users the opportunity to check and verify the policy-making process. Moreover, citizens should have the assurance that their inputs are taken into account by their governors, while governors, by their side, should be assured that user's identity is fully verified and no misuse is allowed. The transparency has to be in some way bidirectional, and the entire process should provide the platform's users significant feedbacks of their contributions (both for governors and citizens).

Open Source software obviously provides a basic level of transparency, by granting access to the application source code. But that's not enough to make users "trust" the platform. A different approach is needed, and this is one of the objectives of this project.

In order to make EUGAGER satisfy the transparency requirement, we will supply the user with an applications results checker. This tool will take as input an application result and will check—by using the toolbox API and directly inquiring raw data—on the correctness of such output. The method on which the checker will stand could be a formal specification of the application behaviour.

Moreover, EUGAGER will implement a set of primitives to enable Tool creators to implement their applications as "secure" tools within the toolbox. By using a home-banking-like approach, and having access to specific methods to user-verify their inputs, a higher level of transparency will be provided to all users.

As about knowledge, the exploitation of the results would be far and wide. Many services offer today broad folksonomies, but the use of this data is limited by our yet limited understanding of their global structure. The possibility to connect a resource with its neighbour resources could be, for example, applied to the entire Internet, suggesting for each page its neighbours in the graph. This will certainly provide an improvement of the feeds provided to the users, leading to a better user experience, and a tool could be developed to investigate the long tail of the World Wide Web: such a tool is still missing. Also, the top-down understanding of a cluster (see par 1.1.3.1, Knowledge Learning) could be used to better understand the different parts of the web. Finally, the understanding of how the different cultures tend to tag elements could also help to understand the evolution of cultures in a measurable way.

> *"Strengthened competitive position of European industry in the field of cooperation platforms"*

EUGAGER will be Open Source Software and will build upon Open Standards used in many other e-participation/e-government projects, facilitating integration and dissemination.

The new tools and services offered by EUGAGER will also give a better visibility on the European research and development at international level, becoming a best practice of good governance applied to industry standards.

Possible scientific findings

The expected results in terms of scientific findings will be outstanding, both in the field of ICT, of Security and of Knowledge. The foreseen research activities performed within the EUGAGER project will focus on issues beyond the state-of-the-art, and the network of Scientific partners from all over the Europe will help to investigate and hopefully solve such issues. Some possible outcomes are expected, for example, in the following areas:

- design of new methodologies for information filtering;

- knowledge learning and tracking methodologies, including tagging systems issues;

- knowledge synthesis and Darwinian systems.

- automatic synthesis of access control policies from end user requirements;

- improvement in authentication procedures and mechanisms;

- design of secure platforms and protocols.

All these expected outcomes should lead to the development of Open Source tools, thus helping to strengthen the European industry in the field of ICT and cooperative platforms.

3.1.2 External Factors and assumptions

Some external factors which could determine whether these impacts will be achieved are the involvement of citizens and of Governments are listed in the following.

Collaboration of the European Governments

Project Stakeholders (especially governments) play a major role on opening up as much data as possible and providing ways for their citizens to interact with it and with other citizens.

With a few exceptions, today there is relatively little collaboration between the e-governments platforms in Europe. Many initiatives have been started by most of the European Member States, but there is not a common standard and a common "language". Our efforts will be devoted to the creation of this common platform, based on Open Standards, to be adopted by each interested Member State, with the aim to reach a huge interoperation between the policy-making processes across Europe. Governments will have also the chance to connect each other to exchange information on common issues. The EUGAGER Project will aim to set up a genuine EU wide cooperation through the pooling of resources and the sharing of activities among most of the Member States and Organisations of the EU. The involvement of the Italian Government (Presidenza del Consiglio dei Ministri) within the EUGAGER project will allow to put the foundations for a wide European collaboration, and we will try to involve other Governments to enlarge the network of users of our platform.

Collaboration of the FLOSS Communities

The early engagement of FLOSS (Free/Libre/Open Source Software) Communities that currently run independent e-participation sites is crucial to create a sustainable development community around the EUGAGER Core. We aim to involve these communities in this project and to convince them to adopt our common framework, for a better interoperation and data exchange between Governments and organizations.

3.1.3 European Approach

We target at creating a platform with the capabilities to become as a *standard de facto* for open government policies and data exchange between users and tools and between tools. Each Member State of the

EU will be able to manage their tools autonomously and, if desired, any group of Member States of the EU will be able to harness the collective intelligence of the platform to extract valuable information. The support of the European Commission to this kind of engagement platform is crucial to communicate to European citizens that their Governments are willing to talk and to reach them. Providing a central place to find tools and activists, EUGAGER will absolutely benefit from a European approach.

From this point of view, the EUGAGER project will give the possibility to enforce International exchanges and cooperation, not only between scientists, but also, as already said, between institutional entities such as local regional and/or national Governments.

3.1.4 Related Activities

Synergies with other European projects are highly desirable; they shall be found in terms of complementarities of objectives and methodologies.

For example, some results of the following Projects will be considered during the development of the EUGAGER Project. A list of such results follows.

- Privacy and Identity Management for Community Services (PICOS, http://www.picos-project.eu/), which has the objective to develop and build a state-of-the-art platform for providing the trust, privacy and identity management aspects of community services and applications on the Internet and in mobile communication networks;
- PRIMELIFE (http://www.primelife.eu/), which has the objective of bringing sustainable privacy and identity management to future networks and services, especially to the Web and its Applications;
- AVANTSSAR (http://www.avantssar.eu/) proposes a rigorous technology for the formal specification and Automated VAlidatioN of Trust and Security of Service-oriented ARchitectures. This technology will be automated into an integrated toolset, the AVANTSSAR Validation Platform, tuned on relevant industrial case studies.
- Trusted Architecture for Securely Shared Services (Tas3, http://www.tas3.eu), which aims to specify a trusted services network that advances the current state of the art of isolated

solutions. It proposes an integrated & context independent solution. This solution consists of checklists, workflows, controls, sample policies and a set of tools to help guide the creation of Tas3 compliant sites and technologies.

Nevertheless, none of these Project address the specific issue of e-participation and e-government platforms, which, as we have explained, encompass more severe requirements to be considered.

Moreover, some Projects have been funded by EU on the field of e-government Platforms, but they address different objectives with respect to EUGAGER. For example:

- The Access-eGov project (http://www.accessegov.org) does not explicitly address Security and Privacy issues. Access-eGov aims at the development and validation of the platform for composition of government services into process definitions, enabling Semantic interoperability of particular e-Government services. The solution is based on the semantic technologies as enhanced WSMO conceptual framework, WSML ontologies, semantic annotation of services, their discovery, composition, mediation, and executing in the SOA environment.

- The R4eGov project (http://www.r4egov.eu) does not explicitly address e-partecipation: it focus mainly on secure exchange of information among public administration, enhancing interoperability between existing administrations: it aims to create secure bridges between national information systems to meet real and anticipated needs of people.

3.2 Dissemination and/or Exploitation of Project Results, and Management of Intellectual Property

3.2.1 Dissemination

The whole WP7100 will be dedicated to the dissemination of the results. This dissemination will be targeted towards the scientific community, towards the general public and towards universities (by publishing booklets for university courses). Another important aspect of the dissemination will be to try to define standards based on the results of EUGAGER.

Dissemination towards the scientific community. Throughout the scientific community , the objective will be to promote EUGAGER tools and services to lead to better networking between scientists in and out of the knowledge, transparency and security research fields, from European Member States.

For that purpose:

- Three scientific EUGAGER conferences will be organised by the partners. The objective will be both to promote the new tools and services of EUGAGER both to call for new papers to better exploit the services offered and the data accessible through these tools. Review papers and papers describing new analyses of results based on multi-disciplinary exchanges will be favoured. This events will include a demonstration of the tools and services developed by EUGAGER.

  In particular, we will present technical and non-technical sessions on the use of EUGAGER, on the following subjects:

  o why Governments should build or migrate their e-participation tools on top of EUGAGER;

  o how they can use Constituency Domains effectively

  o why the European Union should support Governments on the adoption of EUGAGER as a standard and central social networking platform for Citizen Engagement.

  Eventual key partners indentified in the exploitation activities may also be invited to speak about their experience in the project (i.e.: any FLOSS community developing or migrating an application to EUGAGER).

- Regular communications / publications will be sent to scientists to inform about EUGAGER tools and to stimulate new studies. Specific communications will also be realised. This includes publications in scientific and technical journals. Proceedings of each scientific event will be published.

- During the whole duration of the project, the partners will use EUGAGER to better network the e-government research community all over Europe, favouring exchanges between disciplines and countries.

Dissemination towards the general public. As for the general public (including both citizens and governments), the dissemination will aim at enhancing their awareness on the great chances offered by the existence of a platform allowing the empowerment and engagement of all types of societal groups and communities in policy-making processes.

For that purpose, the three public conferences will be organized also for promotion and media attention. The partners will also participate to other existing public events. Specific actions will be undertaken towards the Governments across European Member States, exploiting also he involvement in the EUGAGER project of the Italian Government (Presidenza del Consiglio dei Ministri).

In parallel, the partners will organize several press events and will communicate with journalists to ensure publications in journals and magazines with a large distribution on all the research fields covered by the project.

Also, by using targeted online Advertisement Campaigns from major search engines, we intend to reach a wider audience with straightforward messages to stimulate citizen engagement. These campaigns will use advanced targeting filters to focus on most valuable users (i.e.: target keywords like "Petitions", "Public Activism", "Government 2.0" to focus on interest; exclude non-EU countries to focus on geographical location, etc...).

Finally, a web portal will be implemented, to show the benefits of having a common platform to provide institutional and technical information on the project and a way to aggregate people interested in further development of the Toolbox or new Tools for it (see also exploitation), and the EUGAGER website (i.e.: www.eugager.eu) will host the Toolbox documentation in a wiki-like environment; a bug tracking system and developer mailing list for open source contributions; a regular forum for user support, press releases and general news about the project progress. It will also host the software repository and the source code download link.

3.2.2 Exploitation

The exploitation of the Project results will be addressed by the whole WP7200.

The primary area where the results and services of the EUGAGER project can be exploited is undoubtedly the e-government and e-participation field.

The involvement of the Italian Government, assured by the active participation of the Presidenza del Consiglio dei Ministri within the EUGAGER project, will be the primary way in which our result will be exploited, as we will refer to them primarily as a privileged end-user of our platform.

Moreover, Governments at all levels will be approached to choose EUGAGER as the base platform for their next e-participation and e-governance tools, and/or to migrate existing tools that are not having satisfactory return in terms of citizen participation.

Thanks to our framework, European governments will have on one side a common ICT platform to involve citizens in the so hard and crucial decision-making process. On the other side, cooperation between European countries will be enforced throughout the secure connection between the different platforms.

As a project result, a framework for the development of on-line services for E-Government will be presented. In order to demonstrate the capabilities of our framework, we will implement some applications using the API interface with the platform and giving to the user provable results.

In the long term, we expect to approach businesses interested in learning how to develop or integrate software for the EUGAGER platform, as they can offer services for governments in their home countries, stimulating also local software industry. We will thus exploit the opportunity to offer training sessions to the private companies that are interested in offering such kinds of services.

Finally, we will exploit our network of contact with current and active FLOSS Communities running independent e-participation initiatives and invite them to early adopt EUGAGER as a base platform, to join forces in reaching a critical-mass and eventually transforming it into a one-stop-shop for citizen engagement tools.

In the project, an Exploitation Plan will be prepared. The purpose of this plan is to detail how the tools and services developed within the project can be used for exploiting commercially the results of the project (the Exploitation Plan is effectively a traditional Business Plan, identifying the business markets, performing a SWOT analysis for each market, defining the steps to take to enter into that market successfully).

4   SECTION 4 - ETHICAL ISSUES

Relations with non EU members will follow the framework defined by EU policies such as cooperation policy, neighbourhood policy.

The following table resumes the compliance with ethical rules of EU.

Note that in the case studies experimentation (tasks T7150, T7160, T7170) we will never gather data related to real people, thus we are not processing real personal data (in particular, real political views).

Table 3.2-f - Ethical Issues

	YES	PAGE
Informed Consent		
• Does the proposal involve children?		
• Does the proposal involve patients or persons not able to give consent?		
• Does the proposal involve adult healthy volunteers?		
• Does the proposal involve Human Genetic Material?		
• Does the proposal involve Human biological samples?		
• Does the proposal involve Human data collection?		
Research on Human embryo/foetus		
• Does the proposal involve Human Embryos?		
• Does the proposal involve Human Foetal Tissue / Cells?		
• Does the proposal involve Human Embryonic Stem Cells?		
Privacy		
• Does the proposal involve processing of genetic information or personal data (e.g. health, sexual lifestyle, ethnicity, political opinion, religious or philosophical conviction)		
• Does the proposal involve tracking the location or observation of people?		
Research on Animals		
• Does the proposal involve research on animals?		
• Are those animals transgenic small laboratory animals?		
• Are those animals transgenic farm animals?		
• Are those animals cloned farm animals?		
• Are those animals non-human primates?		
Research Involving Developing Countries		
• Use of local resources (genetic, animal, plant etc)		
• Impact on local community		
Dual Use		
• Research having direct military application		
• Research having the potential for terrorist abuse		
ICT Implants		
• Does the proposal involve clinical trials of ICT implants?		
I CONFIRM THAT NONE OF THE ABOVE ISSUES APPLY TO MY PROPOSAL	YES	

5 SECTION 5 - REFERENCES

Formal Verification

[M:e-gov]"The E-government Handbook for Developing Countries. A project of InfoDev and The Center for Democracy & Technology." Center for Democracy & Technology, Nov 2002, http://www.cdt.org/egov/handbook/2002-11-14egovhandbook.pdf

[M:HMHX07] Vincent C. Hu, Evan Martin, JeeHyun Hwang, and Tao Xie, Conformance Checking of Access Control Policies Specified in XACML, COMPSAC '07, pages 275—280, IEEE Computer Society

[M:ZRG08] Nan Zhang, Mark Ryan, and Dimitar P. Guelev, Synthesising verified access control systems through model checking, J. Comput. Secur., 16(1), 2008, IOS Press

[M:KMW08] Martin Karusseit, Tiziana Margaria, and Holger Willebrandt, Policy expression and checking in XACML, WS-Policies, and the jABC, TAV-WEB '08, pages = 20—26, ACM

[M:ADMP01] Pablo Argon, Giorgio Delzanno, Supratik Mukhopadhyay, and Andreas Podelski, Model Checking Communication Protocols, SOFSEM '01, pages 160—170, Springer-Verlag

[M:MMS97] J. C. Mitchell, M. Mitchell and U. Stern, Automated analysis of cryptographic protocols using Murphi, SP '97, pages 141, IEEE Computer Society

[M:MMS98] J. C. Mitchell, V. Shmatikov and U. Stern, Finite-State Analysis of SSL 3.0, Seventh USENIX Security Symposium, USENIX, 1998, pages 201—216

[M:KKK08] Prabhu Shankar Kaliappan, Hartmut Koenig, Vishnu Kumar Kaliappan, "Designing and Verifying Communication Protocols Using Model Driven Architecture and Spin Model Checker," *Computer Science and Software Engineering, International Conference on*, vol. 2, no. 2, pp. 227-230, 2008 International Conference on Computer Science and Software Engineering, 2008.

[M:XACML-web]   http://www.oasis-open.org/committees/tc_home.php?wg_abbrev=xacml

[M:WSP-web] http://www.w3.org/TR/ws-policy/

[M:RW87] RJ Ramadge and WM Wonham: *Supervisory control of a class of discrete event processes*, SIAM J. Control and Optimization, 25(1), pp. 206-230, 1987

[M:ZS05] Ziller, R. and Schneider, K. 2005. Combining supervisor synthesis and model checking. *Trans. on Embedded Computing Sys.* 4, 2 (May. 2005), 331-362.

[M:AU06]   A   User   Guide   to   HyTech: http://www.eecs.berkeley.edu/_tah/HyTech, 2006.

[M:ABCS04] G. Audemard, M. Bozzano, A. Cimatti, and R. Sebastiani. Verifying industrial hybrid systems with mathsat. Electronic Notes Theoret. Comput. Sci., 89(4), 2004.

[M:ABD+00] E. Asarin, O. Bournez, T. Dang, O. Maler, and A. Pnueli. Effective synthesis of switching controllers for linear systems. Proceedings of the IEEE, 88(7):1011–1025, Jul 2000.

[M:ABG+05] Cyrille Artho, Howard Barringer, Allen Goldberg, Klaus Havelund, Sarfraz Khurshid, Michael R. Lowry, Corina S. Pasareanu, Grigore Rosu, Koushik Sen, Willem Visser, and Richard Washington. Combining test case generation and runtime verification. Theor. Comput. Sci., 336(2-3):209–234, 2005.

[M:ABM04] Rajeev Alur, Mikhail Bernadsky, and P. Madhusudan. Optimal reachability for weighted timed games. In ICALP, pages 122–133, 2004.

[M:ACH+95] R. Alur, C. Courcoubetis, N. Halbwachs, T. A. Henzinger, P. H. Ho, X. Nicollin, A. Olivero, J. Sifakis, and S. Yovine. The algorithmic analysis of hybrid systems. Theoretical Computer Science, 138(1):3 – 34, 1995. Hybrid Systems.

[M:ACMN05] Rajeev Alur, Pavol Cern'y, P. Madhusudan, and Wonhong Nam. Synthesis of interface specifications for java classes. In POPL, pages 98–109, 2005.

[M:ADI06] Rajeev Alur, Thao Dang, and Franjo Ivan˘ci´c. Predicate abstraction for reachability analysis of hybrid systems. ACM Trans. on Embedded Computing Sys., 5(1):152–199, 2006.

[M:AE01] Paul C. Attie and E. Allen Emerson. Synthesis of concurrent programs for an atomic read/write model of computation. ACM Trans. Program. Lang. Syst., 23(2):187–242, 2001.

[M:AHH96] Rajeev Alur, Thomas A. Henzinger, and Pei-Hsin Ho. Automatic symbolic verification of embedded systems. IEEE Trans. Softw. Eng., 22(3):181–201, 1996.

[M:Alu99] Rajeev Alur. Timed automata. In CAV, pages 8–22, 1999.

[M:AM99] Eugene Asarin and Oded Maler. As soon as possible: Time optimal control for timed automata. In HSCC, pages 19–30, 1999.

[M:AM04] Rajeev Alur and P. Madhusudan. Decision problems for timed automata: A survey. In SFM, pages 1–24, 2004.

[M:AMP94] Eugene Asarin, OdedMaler, and Amir Pnueli. Symbolic controller synthesis for discrete and timed systems. In Hybrid Systems, pages 1–20, 1994.

[M:ASY07] Eugene Asarin, Gerardo Schneider, and Sergio Yovine. Algorithmic analysis of polygonal hybrid systems, part i: Reachability. Theoretical Computer Science, 379(1-2):231 – 265, 2007.

[M:BBBM05] F. Borrelli, M. Baotic, A. Bemporad, and M. Morari. Dynamic programming for constrained optimal control of discrete-time linear hybrid systems. Automatica, 41:1709–1721, October 2005.

[M:BBM00] A. Bemporad, F. Borrelli, and M. Morari. Piecewise linear optimal controllers for hybrid systems. American Control Conference, 2000. Proceedings of the 2000, 2:1190–1194 vol.2, 2000.

[M:BBM02] Alberto Bemporad, Francesco Borrelli, and Manfred Morari. On the optimal control law for linear discrete time hybrid systems. In HSCC, pages 105–119, 2002.

[M:BCCZ99] Armin Biere, Alessandro Cimatti, Edmund M. Clarke, and Yunshan Zhu. Symbolic model checking without bdds. In Rance Cleaveland, editor, Tools and Algorithms for Construction and Analysis of Systems, 5th International Conference, TACAS '99, Held as Part of the European Joint Conferences on the Theory and Practice of Software, ETAPS'99, Amsterdam, The Netherlands, March 22-28, 1999, Proceedings, volume 1579 of Lecture Notes in Computer Science, pages 193–207. Springer, 1999.

[M:BG04] Alberto Bemporad and Nicol`o Giorgetti. A sat-based hybrid solver for optimal control of hybrid systems. In HSCC, pages 126–141, 2004.

[M:BM99a] Alberto Bemporad and Manfred Morari. Verification of hybrid systems via mathematical programming. In HSCC, pages 31–45, 1999.

[M:BM99b] Alberto Bemporad and Manfred Morari. Verification of hybrid systems via mathematical programming. In HSCC '99: Proceedings of the Second International Workshop on Hybrid Systems, pages 31–45, London, UK, 1999. Springer-Verlag.

[M:BRH07] Howard Barringer, David E. Rydeheard, and Klaus Havelund. Rule systems for run-time monitoring: From eagleto ruler. In RV, pages 111–125, 2007.

[M:Bro91] William L. Brogan. Modern control theory (3rd ed.). Prentice-Hall, Inc., Upper Saddle River, NJ, USA, 1991.

[M:Cac04]   CachedMurphiWeb   Page: http://www.dsi.uniroma1.it/_tronci/cached.murphi.html, 2004.

[M:CE81] Edmund M. Clarke and E. Allen Emerson. Design and synthesis of synchronization skeletons using branching-time temporal logic. In Logic of Programs, pages 52–71, 1981.

[M:DDM04] Thao Dang, Alexandre Donz´e, and Oded Maler. Verification of analog and mixed-signal circuits using hybrid system techniques. In FMCAD, pages 21–36, 2004.

[M:DIM+03] G. Della Penna, B. Intrigila, I. Melatti, M. Minichino, E. Ciancamerla, A. Parisse, E. Tronci, and M. Venturini Zilli. Automatic verification of a turbogas control system with the murphi verifier. In Oded Maler and Amir Pnueli, editors, Hybrid Systems: Computation and Control, 6th Inter- national Workshop, HSCC 2003 Prague, Czech Republic, April 3-5, 2003, Proceedings, volume 2623 of Lecture Notes in Computer Science, pages 141–155. Springer, 2003.

[M:DIM+04] G. Della Penna, B. Intrigila, I. Melatti, E. Tronci, and M. Venturini Zilli. Exploiting transition locality in automatic verification of finite state concurrent systems. STTT, 6(4):320–341, 2004.

[M:DIM+06] G. Della Penna, B. Intrigila, D. Magazzeni, I. Melatti, A. Tofani, and E. Tronci. Automatic generation of optimal controllers through model checking techniques. In ICINCO 2006, Proceedings of the 3rd International Conference on Informatics in Control, Automation and Robotics, 2006. INSTICC Press, 2006.

[M:ECZ01] R. Raimi E. Clarke, A. Biere and Y. Zhu. Bounded model checking using satisfiability solving. Formal Methods in system Design, 19:7–34, July 2001.

[M:EFH08] Andreas Eggers, Martin Fr"anzle, and Christian Herde. Sat modulo ode: A direct sat approach to hybrid systems. In ATVA, pages 171–185, 2008.

[M:FH07] Martin Fr"anzle and Christian Herde. Hysat: An efficient proof engine for bounded model checking of hybrid systems. Formal Methods in System Design, 30(3):179–198, 2007.

[M:FMO99] Martin Fr"anzle and Markus M"uller-Olm. Compilation and synthesis for real-time embedded controllers. In Correct System Design, pages 256–287, 1999.

[M:Fre08] Goran Frehse. Phaver: algorithmic verification of hybrid systems past hytech. Int. J. Softw. Tools Technol. Transf., 10(3):263–279, 2008.

[M:GPB05] N. Giorgetti, G. J. Pappas, and A. Bemporad. Bounded model checking of hybrid dynamical systems. In CDC '05: Proceedings of the 44th IEEE International Conference on Decision and Control, Washington, DC, USA, 2005. IEEE Computer Society.

[M:HCY03] Alan J. Hu, Jeremy Casas, and Jin Yang. Efficient generation of monitor circuits for gste assertion graphs. In ICCAD, pages 154–160, 2003.

[M:HEFT08] Christian Herde, Andreas Eggers, Martin Fr"anzle, and Tino Teige. Analysis of hybrid systems using hysat. In ICONS, pages 196–201, 2008.

[M:HHWT97] T.A. Henzinger, P.-H. Ho, and H. Wong-Toi. Hytech: A model checker for hybrid systems. Software Tools for Technology Transfer, 1(1):110–122, Dec. 1997.

[M:HK97] Thomas A. Henzinger and Peter W. Kopke. Discrete-time control for rectangular hybrid automata. In ICALP, pages 582–593, 1997.

[M:HKPV95] Thomas A. Henzinger, Peter W. Kopke, Anuj Puri, and Pravin Varaiya. What's decidable about hybrid automata? In STOC '95: Proceedings of the twenty-seventh annual ACM symposium on Theory of computing, pages 373–382, New York, NY, USA, 1995. ACM.

[M:HR02] Klaus Havelund and Grigore Rosu. Synthesizing monitors for safety properties. In TACAS, pages 342–356, 2002.

[M:HR04] Klaus Havelund and Grigore Rosu. Efficient monitoring of safety properties. STTT, 6(2):158–173, 2004.

[M:HS06] Tom Henzinger and Joseph Sifakis. The embedded systems design challenge. In Proceedings of the 14th International Symposium on Formal Methods (FM), Lecture Notes in Computer Science. Springer. August 2006.

[M:HYS06] Hysdel Web Page: http://control.ee.ethz.ch/ hybrid/hysdel/, 2006.

[M:IMT07] B. Intrigila, I. Melatti, and E. Tronci. Automatic synthesis of robust numerical controllers. Autonomic and Autonomous Systems, 2007. ICAS07. Third International Conference on, pages 4–4, June 2007.

[M:JKWC07] Sumit Kumar Jha, Bruce H. Krogh, James E. Weimer, and Edmund M. Clarke. Reachability for linear hybrid automata using iterative relaxation abstraction. In HSCC, pages 287–300, 2007.

[M:KMTV00] Orna Kupferman, P. Madhusudan, P. S. Thiagarajan, and Moshe Y. Vardi. Open systems in reactive environments: Control and synthesis. In CONCUR, pages 92–107, 2000.

[M:LPY97] Kim G. Larsen, Paul Pettersson, and Wang Yi. Uppaal: Status and developments. In Orna Grumberg, editor, Computer Aided Verification, 9th International Conference, CAV '97, Haifa, Israel, June 22-25, 1997, Proceedings, volume 1254 of Lecture Notes in Computer Science, pages 456–459. Springer, 1997.

[M:Mat07] MatSAT Web Page: http://mathsat.itc.it/, 2007.

[M:MKM02] Oded Maler, Bruce H. Krogh, and Moez Mahfoudh. On control with bounded computational resources. In FTRTFT, pages 147–164, 2002.

[M:MN04] Oded Maler and Dejan Nickovic. Monitoring temporal properties of continuous signals. In FORMATS/FTRTFT, pages 152–166, 2004.

[M:MNP07] Oded Maler, Dejan Nickovic, and Amir Pnueli. On synthesizing controllers from bounded-response properties. In CAV, pages 95–107, 2007.

[M:MPS95] Oded Maler, Amir Pnueli, and Joseph Sifakis. On the synthesis of discrete controllers for timed systems (an extended abstract). In STACS, pages 229–242, 1995.

[M:MT02] P. Madhusudan and P. S. Thiagarajan. Branching time controllers for discrete event systems. Theor. Comput. Sci., 274(1-2):117–149, 2002.

[M:MT07] Federico Mari and Enrico Tronci. Cegar based bounded model checking of discrete time hybrid systems. In HSCC, pages 399–412, 2007.

[M:NHY04] Kelvin Ng, Alan J. Hu, and Jin Yang. Generating monitor circuits for simulation-friendly gste assertion graphs. In ICCD, pages 409–416, 2004.

[M:NPAG06] Truong Nghiem, George J. Pappas, Rajeev Alur, and Antoine Girard. Timetriggered implementations of dynamic controllers. In EMSOFT, pages 2–11, 2006.

[M:OH02] Marcio T. Oliveira and Alan J. Hu. High-level specification and automatic generation of ip interface monitors. In DAC, pages 129–134, 2002.

[M:PC07] Andr´e Platzer and Edmund M. Clarke. The image computation problem in hybrid systems model checking. In HSCC, pages 473–486, 2007.

[M:PMT+08] G. Della Penna, D. Magazzeni, A. Tofani, B. Intrigila, I. Melatti, and E. Tronci. Automated Generation of Optimal Controllers through Model Checking Techniques, volume 15 of Lecture Notes in Electrical Engineering. Springer, June 2008.

[M:PR89] Amir Pnueli and Roni Rosner. On the synthesis of a reactive module. In POPL, pages 179–190, 1989.

[M:SEK03] Matthew Senesky, Gabriel Eirea, and Tak-John Koo. Hybrid modelling and control of power electronics. In Hybrid Systems:

Computation and Control (HSCC), volume 2623 of Lecture Notes in Computer Science, pages 450–465, Prague, Czech Republic, April 2003. Springer.

[M:TA99] Stavros Tripakis and Karine Altisen. On-the-fly controller synthesis for discrete and dense-time systems. In World Congress on Formal Methods, pages 233–252, 1999.

[M:TB04] F.D. Torrisi and A. Bemporad. HYSDEL — A tool for generating computational hybrid models for analysis and synthesis problems. IEEE Transactions on Control System Technology, 12(2):235–249, mar 2004.

[M:TGP04] Paulo Tabuada, George, and J. Pappas. G.j.: Linear time logic control of linear systems. IEEE Transaction on Automatic Control, 2004.

[M:Tro96] Enrico Tronci. Optimal finite state supervisory control. In CDC '96: Proceedings of the 35th IEEE International Conference on Decision and Control, Washington, DC, USA, 1996. IEEE Computer Society.

[M:Tro97] Enrico Tronci. On computing optimal controllers for finite state systems. In CDC '97: Proceedings of the 36th IEEE International Conference on Decision and Control, Washington, DC, USA, 1997. IEEE Computer Society.

[M:Tro98] Enrico Tronci. Automatic synthesis of controllers from formal specifications. In ICFEM '98: Proceedings of the Second IEEE International Conference on Formal Engineering Methods, page 134, Washington, DC, USA, 1998. IEEE Computer Society.

[M:Tro99a] Enrico Tronci. Automatic synthesis of control software for an industrial automation control system. In ASE '99: Proceedings of the 14th IEEE international conference on Automated software engineering, page 247,Washington, DC, USA, 1999. IEEE Computer Society.

[M:Tro99b] Enrico Tronci. Formally modeling a metal processing plant and its closed loop specifications. In HASE '99: The 4th IEEE International Symposium on High-Assurance Systems Engineering, page 151, Washington, DC, USA, 1999. IEEE Computer Society.

[M:TY01] Stavros Tripakis and Sergio Yovine. Timing analysis and code generation of vehicle control software using taxys. Electr. Notes Theor. Comput. Sci., 55(2), 2001.

[M:WT97] H. Wong-Toi. The synthesis of controllers for linear hybrid automata. In 36th IEEE Conf. on: Decision and Control(CDC), volume 5, pages 4607–4612 vol.5, Dec 1997.

[M:PCC96] G.C. Necula, Proof-Carrying Code, Proceeding of POPL 97, ACM.

Security

[S:XACML05] MOSES, T. eXtensible Access *Control Markup Language (XACML) Version 2.0. Standard*, Organization for the Advancement of Structured Information Standards (OASIS), February 2005   http://docs.oasisopen.org/xacml/2.0/access   control-xacml-2.0-core-spec-os.pdf

[S:MAZ04] Paul J. Mazzuca, *Access Control in a Distributed Decentralized Network: An XML Approach to Network Security using XACML and SAML,* Dartmouth Computer Science Technical Report TR2004-506, Spring 2004.

[S:EML08] Oasis, *The Case for using Election Markup Language (EML),*   9   January   2008,   http://www.oasis-open.org/committees/download.php/26747/The%20Case%20for%20EML%20v2.pdf

[S:VOT04] *Legal, Operational and Technical standards For e-voting, Recommendation Rec(2004)11 adopted by the Committee of Ministers of the Council of Europe on 30 September 2004 and explanatory memorandum*, April 2005,
http://www.coe.int/t/e/integrated_projects/democracy/02_activities/02_e%2Dvoting/01_recommendation/Rec(2004)11_Eng_Evoting_and_Expl_Memo.pdf

[S:AEGOV07] *Access to e-Government Services Employing Semantic Technologies, D3.2 Access-eGov Components Functional Descriptions*, FP6-2004-27020 Access-eGov, March 2007
http://www.accessegov.org/acegov/uploadedFiles/webfiles/cffile_6_2_06_3_35_24_PM.pdf

[S:BJR06] Brainard, Juels, Rivest, Szydlo, Yung, *Fourth Factor Authentication: Somebody You Know*, CCS'06, October 30–November 3, 2006, Alexandria,Virginia, USA

[S:IDMAN08] National Science and Technology Council, Subcommittee on Biometrics and Identity Management, *Identity Management Task Force Report 2008*, http://www.biometrics.gov/Documents/IdMReport_22SEP08_Final.pdf

[S:LEW08] James A. Lewis, *Authentication 2.0 - New Opportunities for Online Identification*, Center for Strategic and International Studies, January 2008,
http://www.csis.org/media/csis/pubs/080115_authentication.pdf

[S:JOS05] Jøsang, A., Fabre, J., Hay, B., Dalziel, J., and Pope, S. 2005. *Trust requirements in identity management*, In Proceedings of the 2005 Australasian Workshop on Grid Computing and E-Research - Volume 44 (Newcastle, New South Wales, Australia).

[S:VOL07] Volkamer, Melanie; McGaley, Margaret. *Requirements and Evaluation Procedures for eVoting*, Availability, Reliability and Security, 2007. ARES 2007. The Second International Conference on, 10-13 April 2007 Page(s):895 – 902

[S:CET08] Cetinkaya, O., *Analysis of Security Requirements for Cryptographic Voting Protocols (Extended Abstract)*, Availability, Reliability and Security, 2008. ARES 08. Third International Conference on, 4-7 March 2008 Page(s):1451 – 1456

[S:SHI09] Shibboleth® Home Page, http://shibboleth.internet2.edu/

[S:KER94] B. Clifford Neuman and Theodore Ts'o. *Kerberos: An Authentication Service for Computer Networks*, IEEE Communications, 32(9):33-38. September 1994

[S:OPID09], OpenID Home Page, http://openid.net/

[S:SAM06]. R. Sampigethaya, and R. Poovendran, *A framework and taxonomy for comparison of electronic voting schemes,* Elsevier Computers & Security, Vol. 25, No. 2, pp. 137-153, 2006.

[S:OAUTH06], OAuth Core 1.0, http://oauth.net/core/1.0/

[S:KMP02], Manuel Koch, Luigi V. Mancini, Francesco Parisi-Presicce, *A graph-based formalism for RBAC*. ACM Trans. Inf. Syst. Secur. 5(3): 332-365 (2002)

[S:KMP05] Manuel Koch, Luigi V. Mancini, Francesco Parisi-Presicce: *Graph-based specification of access control policies*. J. Comput. Syst. Sci. 71(1): 1-33 (2005)

Web 2.0

[W:CA07] Anderson, Chris. The Long Tail: How Endless Choice Is Creating Unlimited Demand. Random House ,2007.

[W:SJ05] Surowiecki, James. The Wisdom of Crowds. Random House, 2005.

[W:tech-web] http://technorati.com/blogging/state-of-the-blogosphere/

[W:wired-web] http://blog.wired.com/business/2009/03/government-agen.html

[W:web2-web] http://www.oreillynet.com/pub/a/oreilly/tim/news/2005/09/30/what-is-web-20.html

[W:metagov-web] http://www.metagovernment.org

[W:wh-web] http://whitehouse2.org/

[W:tgde-web] http://tgde.org/

[W:dec-web] http://www.decidiamo.it/

[W:wh-q-web] http://www.whitehouse.gov/OpenForQuestions/

[W:fb-web] http://wiki.developers.facebook.com/index.php/Main_Page

[W:opensoc-web] http://code.google.com/apis/opensocial/

[W:gmpg-web] http://gmpg.org/xfn/faq

[W:foaf-web] http://www.foaf-project.org/docs/specs

[W:rst-web] http://en.wikipedia.org/wiki/Representational_State_Transfer

[W:cnipa-web]http://www.cnipa.gov.it/site/it-IT/Attivit%C3%A0/E-gov_per_Regioni_ed_Enti_locali/Monitoraggio_PAL/Progetti_e-democracy/

[W:techcr-web] http://www.techcrunch.com/2008/05/15/he-said-she-said-in-google-v-facebook/

[W:fc-web] http://www.google.com/friendconnect/

[W:fbc-web] http://wiki.developers.facebook.com/index.php/Facebook_Connect

[W:dfnh-web]
http://www.democracyfornewhampshire.com/node/view/6278
[w:Spa05] Giovani Spagnolo, O Software Livre como Modelo de Negócios, EDUCON/NAIPPE/Universidade de São Paulo (USP), 2005, http://www.scribd.com/doc/11515318/20032005-O-Software-Livre-como-Modelo-de-Negocios-Monografia-de-Conclusao-MBA-Executivo-em-Gestao-Empresarial-Estrategica-EDUCONNAIPPE-USP

Synthesis and Tags

[K:TP08] Taylor and Pacelli. Mathematics and Politics: Strategy, Voting, Power and Proof. springer book (2008)

[K:C07] Cattuto et al. From the Cover: Semiotic dynamics and collaborative tagging. Proceedings of the National Academy of Sciences (2007) vol. 104 (5) pp. 1461-1464

[K:C08] Cattuto et al. Semantic Analysis of Tag Similarity Measures in Collaborative Tagging Systems. arXiv (2008) vol. cs.DL

[K:M08] Jason Morrison. Tagging and searching: Search retrieval effectiveness of folksonomies on the World Wide Web. Information Processing and Management (2008) vol. 44 pp. 1562-1579

[K:SC08] Sinclair and Cardew-Hall. The folksonomy tag cloud: when is it useful?. Journal of Information Science (2008),

[K:S08] Seifert et al. On the Beauty and Usability of Tag Clouds. 12th International Conference Information Visualisation (2008),

[K:B08] Bateman et al. Seeing things in the clouds: the effect of visual features on tag cloud selections. Proceedings of the nineteenth ACM conference on Hypertext (2008),

[K:KL07] Kaser and Lemire. Tag-Cloud Drawing: Algorithms for Cloud Visualization. Arxiv preprint cs.DS (2007)

[K:M05] Mika. Ontologies are us: A unified model of social networks and semantics. The Semantic Web – ISWC 2005 (2005) vol. 3729/2005 pp. 522-536

Recommendation Techniques

[B:AK07] G. Adomavicius, Y. Kwon, *New Recommendation Techniques for Multi-Criteria Rating Systems*, IEEE Intelligent Systems, Special Issue on Recommender Systems, 20(3), 2007

[B:AT05] G. Adomavicius, A. Tuzhilin, *Toward the Next Generation of Recommender Systems: A Survey of the State-of-the-Art and Possible Extensions*, IEEE Transactions on Knowledge And Data Engineering, Vol 17, No. 6, June 2005

[B:BHK98] J. S. Breese, D. Heckerman, C. Kadie, *Empirical Analysis of Predictive Algorithms for Collaborative Filtering*, Proceedings of the Fourteenth Conference on Uncertainty in Artificial Intelligence (UAI-98). San Francisco : Morgan Kaufmann, 1998, S. 43-52

[B:GWC04] M. Gnasa, M. Won, A. B. Cremers, *Three pillars for congenial web search. Continuous evaluation for enhancing web search effectiveness*. Journal ofWeb Engineering 3 (2004) 252–280

[B:KGC06] S. M. Kirsch, M. Gnasa, A. B. Cremers, *Beyond the web: Retrieval in social information spaces*. In Proceedings of the 28th European Conference on Information Retrieval (ECIR 2006), 2006.

[B:MGT+87] T. W. Malone, K. R. Grant, F. A. Turbak, S. A. Brobst, M. D. Cohen, *Intelligent information-sharing systems*, Commun. ACM 30 (1987), Nr. 5, S. 390-402. - ISSN 0001-0782

[B:PP04] M. Papagelis, D. Plexousakis, *Qualitative Analysis of User-Based and Item-Based Prediction Algorithms for Recommendation Agents*. CIA, 2004, S. 152-166

[B:RIS+94] P. Resnick, N. Iacovou, M. Suchak, P. Bergstorm, J. Riedl, GroupLens: *An Open Architecture for Collaborative Filtering of Netnews*. Proceedings of ACM 1994 Conference on Computer Supported Cooperative Work. Chapel Hill, North Carolina : ACM, 1994, S. 175{186

[B:RV97] P. Resnick, H. Varian: *Recommender Systems (introduction to special section). Communications of the ACM*, March 1997 Bd. 40(3), 1997

[B:S71] G. Salton, *The SMART Retrieval System – Experiments in Automatic Document* Processing. Prentice Hall Inc., Englewood Cliffs, NJ, 1971

[B:SK02] J. B. Schafer, J. A. Konstantin, J. Riedl *Meta-recommendation systems: User-controlled integration of diverse recommendations*. Proceedings of the 11th International Conference on Information and Knowledge Management, Nov. 2002, 43–51.

Afterword

After submission, we received our first communication from the EU Commission, stating that 50 proposals were submitted under "ICT for Governance and Policy Modelling". On July 1st 2009 we received the final evaluation from the Commission's reviewers. It read as follows:

- - -

1.Scientific and/or technological excellence (relevant to the topics addressed by the call) (Threshold 3.0/5 ; Weight 1.00)

Mark: 3.0

The proposal presents an approach of a web-based extensible framework for e-participation tools and addresses the objectives of the call concerning Governance and Participation Toolbox. The concept has strong focus on security technologies. However, it does not consider other e-governance aspects in detail.

The proposal indicates potential progress beyond state of the art in specific technology areas, such as information filtering, the application of Web2.0 techniques to cover e-government issues progress beyond state-of-the-art can be expected, or application of model checking techniques.

However, it fails to properly show innovation in participatory e-governance environments at a broader scale. Moreover, it misses to point out, why e.g. model checking technique in this application domain is superior over other existing approaches.

The proposal presents a detailed work plan. The methodology proposed is well suited for the intended work as far as the technology development is concerned. In contrast, only little information is provided considering user requirements, and user test beds.

2.Quality and efficiency of the implementation and the management (Threshold 3.0/5 ; Weight 1.00)

Mark: 3.0

The chosen management structure is appropriate for the type of project. The proposal provides some relevant management aspects, however, it misses to clearly address others or give clear procedures on how to conduct, i.e. for risk management, decision taking, and conflict solution. No well stated strategy is provided how test users will be incorporated in. The consortium partners provide the relevant experience they need for their specific working tasks. The consortium is balanced for the task they want to achieve. From a broader perspective, however, a partner from the application domain is missing who can research, evaluate, and improve the use of the prototype in the area of e-participation and e-governance.

With respect to the addressed development, the allocated resources are acceptable.

However, very little portion of the resources are considered for (especially user) requirement analysis or other user centric activities.

3.The potential impact through the development, dissemination and use of project
results (Threshold 3.0/5 ; Weight 1.00)

Mark: 2.5

The proposal is heavily technology driven. It offers free access to results in terms of OSS, documentation etc, which may increase the impact expected. However, in the context of e-governance, quite little success is visible if only a technology push is present.

The dissemination plan is lacking details. For example, it stays unclear how the consortium will approach which governmental organisations (except for the Presidenza del Consiglio dei Ministri) or citizens (except for advertisement campaigns from search engines). The exploitation activities are described in a vague manner. No concrete measures are proposed.

The proposal failed to clearly address IPR issues. Even in case of full OSS provision, handling of background knowledge and other relevant individual partner assets should be taken into account.

4.Remarks (Threshold 10.0/15)
Total: 8.50
The proposal scored below threshold on Criterion 3.

Does this proposal have ethical issues that need further attention? (If yes, please complete an ethical issues report form (EIR))
N

Note: For each criterion under examination, score values are interpreted as follows:

0- The proposal fails to address the criterion under examination or cannot be judged due to missing or incomplete information; 1- Poor. The criterion is addressed in an inadequate manner, or there are serious inherent weaknesses.; 2- Fair. While the proposal broadly addresses the criterion, there are significant weaknesses.; 3- Good. The proposal addresses the criterion well, although improvements would be necessary.; 4- Very Good. The proposal addresses the criterion very well, although certain improvements are still possible.; 5- Excellent. The proposal successfully addresses all relevant aspects of the criterion in question. Any shortcomings are minor.

- - -

We acknowledge that our proposal can be improved in many ways, and this is the main reason we decided to make it available for anyone with similar ideas about developing a Free/Open Source Citizen Engagement Platform. We think that the potential impact through the development, dissemination and use of the EUGAGER project's results could help Europe to be truly united.

The European Union should strongly consider the fact that today's net citizens spend most of their spare time using social networking sites and Web 2.0 services, and that proprietary solutions like Facebook, Google+, Hi5, Orkut, Twitter and the like just don't suit the needs and transparency requirements of serious governmental applications.

It is also important to see the whole process in a more global framework. Since Obama's election as President of the United States there was a strong impulse for e-government in the United States. This is taking a three-forked path. On the one hand there is a level of transparency, where data from the government are made available to the general population. Then there is a level of e-bureaucracy, where citizens have the possibility of completing general paperwork online. But in addition to all this, there is now research that focuses on how the government should connect with the general population to (a) receive feedback about laws that are about to be adopted; (b) receive ideas and possible solutions to identified problems, and (c) receive indications as to which open problems should be addressed. Those three lines of research all point toward a stronger integration between the population and the government.

We feel that this whole process is very important. It should not just involve the United States, but should involve Europe too. The idea of the government as a platform is being discussed in US for some time now. The EUGAGER platform had similar aims for European countries. Although the plan for EUGAGER was developed independently, multiple sources seem to have reached similar conclusions. Our aim was to ensure that Europe did not fall behind. In a globalised society, good practices are reproduced around the world.

Now, the ultimate goal we are trying to reach by releasing this book is to let some of those ideas flourish around the world. Our hope is that they may return to us improved, hopefully very soon.

http://twitter.com/eugager

http://eugager.tvgio.com

www.ingramcontent.com/pod-product-compliance
Lightning Source LLC
Chambersburg PA
CBHW070948050326
40689CB00014B/3387